"You don't have to be a fan of,  or
Who to appreciate these well-t(g
helpers who rely not only on t t
also on learning from their con ,.
Be prepared to see connections ....o aiiu Cybermen,
and resurrection and regeneration; nuances of gender roles; and
jargon-free discussions of Paul's own writings and later additions."

—JONATHAN H. HARWELL
Rollins College, co-editor of *Theology and Prince*

"In this book, Jeff Nelson answers the question a select few have
longed to see answered: what happens if you compare the lives,
activities, and values of the Doctor and the Apostle Paul? For those
who never thought to ask this question, his book is all the more interesting and valuable, since it opens up fascinating avenues along
which you'll better appreciate your faith and fandom—whether as
a Whovian, a Christian, or both—and at the same time be led to
ask new questions that will deepen your understanding of stories
and/or letters that you think you're familiar with."

—JAMES F. MCGRATH
Clarence L. Goodwin Chair in New Testament Language
and Literature, Butler University

"If you could take the Tardis to Tarsus, what would you learn? If this
question has you intrigued, Jeff Nelson is your trustworthy guide.
A feast for *Doctor Who* fans, and a generative space for students of
the Apostle Paul, this book lives up to its claim to mine the intersections of history, culture, ethics, and faith in ways that make both the
show and the Bible more relevant and fun for everyday life."

—DEBORAH KRAUSE
President and Professor of New Testament,
Eden Theological Seminary

"Jeff Nelson's *The Doctor and the Apostle* left me with a deeper appreciation of *Doctor Who* and a better understanding of the Apostle Paul—both of which I have complicated relationships with. Nelson's unique approach to the intersections of pop culture and the Christian understanding of the Christian biblical canon will enable you to peer into the similarities of science fiction and Scripture. I'm sure you will find yourself in the pages of this book in ways you hadn't thought possible. It's worth your time."

—ROBERT W. LEE
Author of *A Sin by Any Other Name:*
Reckoning with Racism and the Heritage of the South

The Doctor and the Apostle

The Doctor and the Apostle

Intersections Between Doctor Who
and the Letters of Paul

JEFFREY A. NELSON

WIPF & STOCK · Eugene, Oregon

THE DOCTOR AND THE APOSTLE
Intersections Between Doctor Who and the Letters of Paul

Wipf & Stock
An Imprint of Wipf and Stock Publishers
199 W. 8th Ave., Suite 3
Eugene, OR 97401

www.wipfandstock.com

PAPERBACK ISBN: 978-1-7252-6317-8
HARDCOVER ISBN: 978-1-7252-6315-4
EBOOK ISBN: 978-1-7252-6318-5

Manufactured in the U.S.A.   08/06/20

For Chris and Gavin, who know best what this led to.

"Laugh hard. Run fast. Be kind."

—THE TWELFTH DOCTOR

Contents

Acknowledgments

I WROTE THE BULK of this book under some very interesting personal and professional circumstances. I was in the middle of a job transition, and my family and I were as caught up as everyone else in concerns over the coronavirus. It was challenging at times to keep my focus for this project. I drew support from a wide variety of people to remain centered, both for purposes of writing and for the strange context in which I had to complete it.

I am grateful once again to Matthew Wimer, Daniel Lanning, George Callihan, and the rest of the team at Wipf and Stock for their aid and guidance in each step of the publishing process. It was a pleasure to work with you all again.

Thank you as always to my family for their gifts of patience and time as I stole away to write, and for their ongoing love.

I had so many people loving and praying me through my changing of ministry positions, among them Ian Borton, Mindy Quellhorst, Elizabeth Dilley, George Miller, Mike and Jeanne Murawski, Alex and Hope Molozaiy, Brian Burke, Gayle Tucker, and the group known best as The Cohort. Thank you as well to my Community of Practice clergy group: Melody Ward, Gene McAfee, Allen Kahler, Steve Hockstra, Brent Gundlah, and Adam Marquette. I am glad to have so many companions with whom to share this journey with all its twists and turns.

Thank you to the people of Grace United Church of Christ, who got to hear more than their fair share of pop culture references

Acknowledgments

on Sunday mornings over the years, including a few from *Doctor Who* that turned out to be the earliest seeds for this book.

And a thank you to Daniel for introducing me to The Doctor all those years ago. I hope that you're doing well, wherever you are.

1

Fifteen Lives and Two Universes

I SOMETIMES SAY THAT I was a *Doctor Who* fan before I realized it. When I was in elementary school, I was hanging out with a friend at his house. Our relationship had begun thanks to a mutual love of science fiction and fantasy, especially *Ghostbusters*. But that day he was eager to show me some episodes of a show he'd recorded, which featured a strangely dressed man who could travel through time and space in a blue police call box that was noticeably much bigger on the inside.

The man only went by the name The Doctor. In these particular episodes, his most defining sartorial choices were a long tweed coat and an even longer multicolored scarf. He was joined on his adventures by a young woman named Romana and a robotic dog named K-9. The episode I most clearly remember, and which I have long deemed my definitive first experience of the show, was a series called "Meglos," during which The Doctor tries to foil a shape-shifting alien cactus in its efforts to steal a powerful glowing element known as the Dodecahedron and use it for destructive purposes. My friend showed me other adventures, but this one stood out for reasons that are lost to me.

I do remember loving the fantastical elements of the show, especially The Doctor's ship and the fact that he could regenerate into a new form in order to avoid death. This earliest introduction to the world of *Doctor Who* made a lasting impression, and its mythology found its way into my playtime in many ways.

Given the influence of this show on my imagination, however, I never made much of an effort to watch more than what my friend had on hand at his house. Even more inexplicably, I didn't make it a point to watch when I was older and had easier access to it via reruns on TV or through the library. I didn't even get into the series when it was first revived in 2005, although I can recall a tinge of joy in reliving old memories when its return was announced.

But once I finally decided to delve back into the world of The Doctor a few years later, I remembered everything that I loved about it. When your show's central character can go to any planet and any point in time that they want, there are very few limitations that can be placed on the potential for the predicaments they can get into and the strange figures they can meet. I was past due to get to know the boundless possibilities of action and excitement that *Doctor Who* offered, and just as I had back in my most formative years, I was not disappointed.

All of this is to say that I consider myself a genuine Whovian. I am also a minister with an interest in how popular culture and faith may interact with each other. I've been a fan of Jesus for at least as long as I have been of *Doctor Who*, although I like to think that I've been more committed to the former than the latter over the years.

From a spiritual perspective, the potential for learning about faith through the exploits of The Doctor is rich and deep. The show often reflects on the power of kindness, peace, love, endurance, and working together over and against the use of violence, hatred, intimidation, and destruction. It has explored themes of inequality, racism, oppression, creation care, the interaction of religious belief and science, genocide, fundamentalism, and ethics, among so many other issues that a life of faith should have something to say about, if it is to be in any way useful and relevant.

And that is the premise of this book. There is so much that Christians may be able to learn from *Doctor Who*. I have long thought that pop culture can sometimes be a more accessible onramp for exploring important truths about God, life, service, and community than Sunday worship or Bible study can be. Sometimes this is because the former is just more interesting and engaging. Sometimes it's because the former is more willing to talk plainly about life's complexity and struggles. And sometimes it's just because the former is easier to understand. That sounds like a critique of more traditional expressions of faith, and I suppose that it is. But whatever helps us connect more deeply to the truths that my belief system professes, there seems to be more sense in making use of it than avoiding it.

All of that is why I decided to write about one of my favorite shows in this way. Christians can cull a lot of insight from *Doctor Who* that pertains to their faith journey. Whether you're already a fan or this book is your very first brush with the show, I hope that this is true for you.

OUR PRINCIPAL PLAYERS

I've already begun to explain why I see value in exploring the *Doctor Who* universe for its relevancies to faith. It touches on many subjects that parallel what it means to be a Christian—how to love God and love neighbor in the spirit of the life and ministry of Jesus Christ. The Doctor encounters situations that, while set in fantastic times and places with strange and often non-human characters, nevertheless have the basic questions and dilemmas of life at their core. These include how to treat those who are different from us, whether to solve disputes using violence or more peaceful means, what it looks like to trust or hope when you can't clearly anticipate an outcome, what it means to rely on others and live in community, and how it looks to believe in others' redemption even if they are unable to do so themselves.

There is also the figure of The Doctor him—or herself, and the growth, conflict, change, failures, and successes that the viewer is able to watch them experience. Far from being an omniscient or all-powerful character, The Doctor experiences many flaws and struggles. In more than one instance, The Doctor describes themselves as just a traveler who stops in and helps people the best that they can, while learning along the way as much as any other character on the show.

As will be explored throughout the book, these lessons do not often come easily. Part of what makes The Doctor such a compelling character is that they are completely immersed in the situation. They choose to insert themselves in mystery, conflict, and danger, and they react to it with as much fascination, frustration, anger, joy, curiosity, and wonder as anyone else would in a similar predicament. They have the benefit of having lived so long and seen so much that they usually have the knowledge and wisdom to eventually get themselves out of it, but not before deepening their understanding along the way.

For those less familiar with the show, a few basic facts are appropriate to share about The Doctor and the universe in which they reside. The Doctor is an alien from the planet Gallifrey, who is able to travel through time and space thanks to their ship, the TARDIS, which looks like an old British police box. They often travel with one or more companions who are usually human, although there have been some rare exceptions to that over the years.

The Doctor has had at least fourteen different faces since the show's debut. This is due to a special power that The Doctor's species, the Time Lords, came up with known as regeneration, which is triggered when one of their kind suffers a fatal injury. Rather than dying, they morph into a new body with a fresh lifespan, although the length of that lifespan is mostly undefined.

As a result, The Doctor has taken on a variety of personalities and stylistic choices. At times The Doctor has been more gruff and standoffish, and at times more whimsical and compassionate. They have been more grandfatherly and they have been more of a peer or romantic interest. They have been more inquisitive and they have been more confident, even arrogant, about their own intellectual ability.

For these reasons and more, fans of the show often have their favorite incarnations of The Doctor. Viewers gravitate toward certain mixtures of personality and physical traits, and may prefer one or more Doctors over others. Since The Doctor does not have a known name besides this title, the common way to refer to each version of the character is by numerical order, beginning with William Hartnell as the title character in the show's debut: he is The First Doctor, Patrick Troughton The Second Doctor, and so on through the current Thirteenth Doctor, played by Jodie Whittaker. The one exception is when John Hurt was introduced as a non-sequential version of The Doctor for the fiftieth anniversary episode, "The Day of the Doctor"; he is known as The War Doctor.

That should be enough to get the reader started. Much more about the character and the show will, of course, be explored in the chapters ahead.

That brings us to our other main figure in this book, the Apostle Paul. Some may be wondering why I might choose to focus on his specific contributions to the Bible and to Christianity rather than a more generalized exploration of Christian faith. I have a few different answers to that.

First, I think that Paul is a much richer and fascinating person than some may give him credit for being, and that includes both devotees and detractors. The former tend to see him as a sagely and steadfast keeper of the faith, with wisdom that can be lifted from his writings to apply to modern situations just as cleanly as it was when he first composed them. Entire theological systems have been constructed with his thoughts as a foundation. But this view is always in danger of minimizing his flaws, which he is often honest about in these same writings.

The latter are more prone to see those flaws, as well as how problematic it can be to apply some of his ideas to present-day situations. Some of what is attributed to him concerning the place of women in the church and in society in general have been especially damaging throughout the centuries, and many have left him behind as a result. The ways in which Paul's writings have been used to bully, suppress, exclude, and discriminate have brought him much scorn and dismissal.

I think that the real Paul lives somewhere between these two views. He was certainly far from perfect, and he admits this about himself more than once. His words were also contextual, written for specific situations that were playing out in real time in the communities to which he wrote. While this does not excuse ideas that still may cause harm so many centuries removed, it at least helps us better understand why he said what he said.

Paul is credited with having written thirteen letters contained in the New Testament. Scholars have disputed whether at least some of them actually came from his pen or were written by people either familiar with his ideas or who wanted to add credibility to their own. Due to this dispute and for the sake of simplifying things, this book will focus on those letters considered to be genuine: Romans, 1 and 2 Corinthians, Galatians, Philippians, 1 Thessalonians, and Philemon.

The second reason why I am focusing specifically on Paul is because, for reasons already mentioned, I have not always had a good relationship with Paul's writings myself. I have my own stories of having his writings used in abusive ways, as well as the stories of beloved and trusted friends who have been on the receiving end of weaponized Pauline words, and so I have not always trusted these parts of Scripture as much as others. I have come around on that in more recent years, and this book is the latest step in my own journey to reclaim Paul as part of my own faith tradition.

The final reason why I chose Paul is because I see some similarities between him and The Doctor. They both believe in the potential of the people they're trying to help. They are both travelers who do good as best as they know how, although they're just as prone to getting it wrong while learning from their mistakes. They rejoice with people in times of success and encouragement, and they become angry when they think that people can do better. They both live in some median existence between the legend that others have constructed about them and the imperfections that people hold against them.

The more I thought about this comparison, the more interested I became in writing about it. So that, in a nutshell, is why this book exists.

A FEW ASSUMPTIONS AND DISCLAIMERS

Before we proceed, I want to mention a few assumptions with which I'm approaching this book. The first is one I've already mentioned: I'll be working with the letters of Paul that have been deemed authentic by biblical scholars. A further explanation about that will be provided in another chapter.

Second, I am not a big fan of books that explore faith and pop culture that are heavy on the former and only use the latter as an incidental prop. My view is that if you're going to compare and contrast a system of spiritual belief with some piece of film, television, music, or other art, you need to respect the piece enough to let it speak for itself and then see where it leads as a result.

That is why I use the word "intersections" in the title rather than something like "parallels" or "similarities." This book will explore both *Doctor Who* and Paul each on their own terms, identifying where their respective themes align but also identifying where they differ. I aim to put them in conversation with each other, rather than try to shoehorn one into the other in ways that are uncomfortable or inappropriate.

Third, I must describe my method of using pronouns, which you might have picked up on already. The Doctor has been a man through most of the show's run, but the most recent incarnation is a woman. One of The Doctor's primary antagonists, The Master, has also been a man and a woman at various points. Due to this element of gender fluidity on the show, there will come times where I will use the singular "they," "them," or "their" to refer to these characters, mostly when I am speaking about them in the most general terms as they have existed throughout the show's history. When I am writing about a character's specific incarnation within the context of a particular episode, series, season, or actor or actress's tenure, I will use gender-specific pronouns.

Finally, this disclaimer is more for readers who are already fans. Because *Doctor Who* has had such a long existence, this book will not be an exhaustive treatment of the show. It is very likely that I will only make passing reference to, or ignore entirely, somebody's favorite Doctor, companion, adversary, episode, or season. It was not intentional: I had a manuscript deadline and I only had so much time to watch the show while also writing about it. I did attempt, at least, to get as broad an experience of the show as I could, from both the classic series and the revival that began in 2005. I'm sorry if I end up omitting something that you were hoping to be mentioned. If it helps, I couldn't find a way to work in all of my favorites, either (for instance, there's no mention of the episode "Blink," except this parenthetical note).

THE JOURNEY AHEAD

Now that we've dispensed with introductory disclaimers and explanations, here is where we will be going next.

In chapter 2, I will look at the traveling habits of The Doctor and Paul, as well as their relationships to the institutions that spurred their journeys. In the case of The Doctor, this will be a closer look at the features of their ship, the TARDIS, and how it is often a key factor in their adventures beyond giving them the ability to go from one place to another. For Paul, this will be his profession as a tentmaker and his sometimes tenuous relationship to other church leaders and apostles.

Chapter 3 will explore The Doctor and Paul's struggles with their own sense of identity. The Doctor often has to step back and evaluate who they are, most notably after a regeneration, but at times when they are faced with their own overconfidence and failure as well. Paul's case is similar, as he carries his past as a persecutor of the church with him, as well as other weaknesses that at times hinder his ministry with others.

In chapter 4, I will further explore Paul's admissions of weakness, but also how he drew strength from his sense of God's presence and work in the world as well. Likewise, The Doctor often approaches problems while avoiding conventional solutions such as the use of violence to solve them, which some other characters see as weak. This chapter will ask what true strength looks like, and whether it always has to follow the path that many prefer.

Both The Doctor and Paul had moments when they became frustrated with the behavior of humanity. They both wonder at times why they keep bothering to help people when they often end up acting in such disappointing ways. Chapter 5 will explore this frustration, as well as how they deal with it in order to continue in their respective missions.

Chapter 6 will analyze the question of whether anybody is truly beyond turning their life around from one that is harmful to oneself or others to one that is life-giving. For The Doctor, this question was most often personified in his longtime nemesis, The Master. For Paul, this played out in his ongoing argument with others concerning who got to be part of the new Jesus Movement. As we will see, the answer that each come up with is similar to the other's.

The Doctor and Paul also each dealt with the question of what unity looks like if everyone in a group doesn't all look, think, or act exactly alike. For The Doctor, this question usually came up while dealing with their foes the Cybermen. For Paul, this often centered on the issue of whether non-Jewish believers needed to follow parts of the Mosaic law in order to be considered part of the church. Chapter 7 will focus on how each made room for diversity while seeking a common goal.

One's life and faith journey is not meant to be one traveled alone. The Doctor often has a companion who balances them out and helps them see aspects of a situation that they otherwise would be blind to. Paul also had multiple companions who supported his work in different ways. Chapter 8 will focus on the importance of having fellow travelers to help us do what we can't do by ourselves.

As mentioned earlier in this chapter, one of the biggest causes of Paul's notoriety is some of what is included in his letters concerning the place of women in the church. However, there is much more evidence to suggest how much he valued the voice and work of women alongside him, most notably how often he mentions women as coworkers in his ministry. Likewise, The Doctor has had many indispensable women in their life, including their thirteenth incarnation. Chapter 9 will highlight the importance of women to both figures, as well as the continuing critical role that women play in the life of both the world and the church.

Chapter 10 will explore the concept of regeneration in *Doctor Who*, while comparing and contrasting it with Paul's presentation of how resurrection works. There are similarities between the two, but also major differences. One thing that they have in common, however, is the ongoing hope and assurance that they provide for others.

My hopes for you as you continue reading are multiple. I hope that fans will discover something new about this incredibly imaginative show that we love, and that those less familiar with it may be inspired to give it a chance. I hope that those seeking a greater understanding of Christian spirituality and faith will receive that in even a small way. I hope that fans of Paul may be able to approach him more realistically and that non-fans may find something redemptive. I hope that more than one of these things happens for every reader. And I hope most of all that I've done right by both of this book's main subjects, and that as a result they may each have something to say to you.

2

Tents, Houses, and a Blue Box

THE DOCTOR'S TARDIS IS integral to their ability to do what they do. The name TARDIS is an acronym for Time And Relative Dimension In Space, and, true to its name, it is The Doctor's ship that has the ability to travel both through time and space. Its blue police box exterior is arguably the most iconic symbol of the show: both fans and non-fans alike may be able to recognize and associate it with *Doctor Who*, similar to how other vehicles like the Millennium Falcon, USS Enterprise, and a certain modified DeLorean are associated with their own franchises.

Due to its being so critical to The Doctor's life, the TARDIS is ever present even when it's not on screen. After all, every adventure into which The Doctor and their companions stumble is due to traveling there through this special ship. And, as will be discussed shortly, some of the TARDIS's powers give the characters some abilities even when they're not inside it. It is a part of most episodes even when not featured.

As explained on the show, the TARDIS is a product of Time Lord technology and originated on their home planet of Gallifrey. It is one of many that this civilization has produced, and we occasionally see others at work: The Master has their own that can still disguise itself as various other forms, another renegade Time Lord makes use of numerous TARDIS-like ships in "The War Games," and companion Clara eventually gets her own that looks like a diner from the outside in the episode "Hell Bent," as a few examples.

A big part of The First and Second Doctors' tenures is how the TARDIS had been acquired. The Doctor began traveling after stealing it, which immediately made him a fugitive and outlaw in the eyes of the Time Lords. Near the end of "The War Games" series, The Second Doctor reveals that he'd done so because he'd become bored with life on Gallifrey, and wanted to go and see other parts of the universe and see what positive difference he could make for others.

A point of frustration for The Doctor throughout the show's history has been how bureaucratic and stingy the Time Lords tend to be with their technology. He accuses them of hoarding what they have for themselves rather than using it to help resolve conflicts and fight the many evil forces throughout time and space that destroy and oppress. The Doctor chooses to break their laws against interference and venture out to make a positive difference instead, which brings consequences for him even as the Time Lords admit that he's done a lot of good for people thanks to his initial act of theft. During The Third Doctor's time, this transgression is finally forgiven, allowing him to travel with less secrecy and continue his quest to explore and to give aid to others.

A long-running joke of the series is every new character's reaction when they first step inside the TARDIS. The outside has the appearance of a blue police box, with certain measurable dimensions of so many feet or meters on each side. But it's "bigger on the inside," as many exclaim, with a much larger main control room and sometimes-seen corridors and rooms as well. The Doctor sometimes talks about other places contained within the TARDIS, including rooms for companions to stay in, a wardrobe area, recreational spaces, a library, and even other control rooms that are sometimes used instead of the main one. The perceived limitations of the ship's outer appearance are offset by its immense inward one.

The reason the TARDIS looks like a police call box is because it became stuck that way. All TARDISes have a "Chameleon Circuit," which allows them to take different outer forms to blend in with their surroundings. The Master's TARDIS can still do this, as do others that appear on the show. But during one of The Doctor's earliest missions, his became broken.

The inside, however, has undergone many alterations over the course of the series. Many of the earliest Doctors had the same basic layout in the inside of their ship, which was a simple white control room, sparsely decorated. The interior of later Doctors' ships became more personalized and decorative, with most having a darker and larger space illuminated by blue, green, or orange lighting. The inside has been changed nearly every time that The Doctor has changed, and it is hinted that it is by some combination of The Doctor's preferences and the TARDIS's own ability that this happens.

The abilities of the TARDIS are not confined to its inside. It has some functions that extend beyond its walls and that aid The Doctor and their companions even when they are far from it. Early in the episode "The Fires of Pompeii," The Doctor's companion Donna wonders at how she's able to read the non-English text on buildings and signs. The Doctor explains that it is thanks to the TARDIS's translation circuits, which remain connected with its travelers while they walk around. "We're speaking Latin right now," The Doctor adds, noting that these translation circuits also apply to speaking and hearing the languages of other earthly nationalities and alien species. The TARDIS can also provide oxygen for its passengers to venture outside in open space or on other planets, albeit usually on a limited basis. It sometimes has provided force fields for protection, and has sometimes sent telepathic messages to The Doctor and others as well.

From the beginning, the TARDIS has also displayed its own personality and preferences. As mentioned, this sometimes manifests in its changing the inner appearance. But The Doctor often refers to it as a living entity. The Doctor sometimes talks to it affectionately, at other times argues with it, and interprets its feelings toward other characters. In the 1996 movie, The Doctor takes note of how it seems to be reacting to Grace, noting that it likes her. In "Utopia," Captain Jack Harkness clings to the outside of the TARDIS as it travels, and The Doctor later comments that it was trying to shake him off. In "The Husbands of River Song," a Christmas episode, The Doctor yells at the TARDIS for trying to cheer him up by putting holographic reindeer antlers on his head. When The Doctor finally reunites with the TARDIS after being separated for a while in "The Ghost Monument," she expresses how much she has missed and loves it, then shows admiration for its redecoration efforts once she steps inside.

The TARDIS has a rare opportunity to talk back during the episode "The Doctor's Wife," where early on its energy leaves the console of the ship and inhabits the body of a woman. In this form, the TARDIS is able to predict the future and provide insight for what it has been like to travel with The Doctor over the centuries.

At numerous points, she and The Doctor talk about what their time together has been like from her perspective. This includes looking back on when they first got together, where the TARDIS hints that not only did she allow herself to be stolen, but she also stole him, allowing them both to run away. Later on, The Doctor yells at her for being unreliable and often taking him to places where he doesn't want to go, to which she responds that she has actually been taking him where he needs to go instead. Before the soul of the TARDIS returns to the box, she says two things she's always wanted to say. The first is "Hello, Doctor." The second is "I love you."

The TARDIS is much more than a time machine and a spaceship. It is, in its way, a living being that helps steer The Doctor along certain paths, showing an intuition for what they need. It has opinions and feelings for the characters that ride inside. It remains connected to its passengers and provides assistance even when they're not onboard. It endows its inhabitants with what they need both inside and outside its walls. It is much more than it appears, bigger on the inside in more ways than one.

THE MOVEABLE CHURCH

As much credit as we may give to Paul for helping establish the Christian movement in its earliest years, he did not always have the most cordial relationship with his contemporaries. He was regularly at odds with other leaders and with some within some faith communities for reasons related to theology, inclusion, structure, or just basic personality differences.

The primary issue that shows up in his letters is what we could call "the Gentile question." There were many at the Jesus Movement's founding who believed that to become a follower of Jesus meant following the Mosaic law, which included men becoming circumcised. As this movement began within Judaism, they saw the keeping of established traditions, customs, and commandments as still having a place in this new community.

Paul, however, saw expanding the movement beyond these boundaries as being essential to his sense of call. He describes this at the beginning of his letter to the Galatians:

> You have heard, no doubt, of my earlier life in Judaism. I was violently persecuting the church of God and was trying to destroy it. I advanced in Judaism beyond many among my people of the same age, for I was far more zealous for the traditions of my ancestors. But when God, who had set me apart before I was born and called me through his grace, was pleased to reveal his Son to me, so that I might proclaim him among the Gentiles, I did not confer with any human being, nor did I go up to Jerusalem to those who were already apostles before me, but I went away at once into Arabia, and afterwards I returned to Damascus. (Galatians 1:13–17)

At the beginning of this passage, Paul couches his experience in his life in Judaism. Having had his transformative moment that has led to his newfound sense of purpose, he doesn't divorce himself from what came before so much as describe it as a new direction within it. The "earlier life in Judaism" that he references is his opposition to and persecution of the church; he describes it as a sign of his dedication and devotion to his faith, which he does more than once in his letters.

When he mentions the revelation from God that he has received, he makes no differentiation between the God he previously knew as part of his Jewish faith and some new separate God who sent Jesus. Rather, it is the same God who has given a new understanding of how Jesus is related to what he knew before. In the same sense, he states that God has given him a new purpose: to advance the church's mission rather than try to stop it.

Krister Stendahl points out that when Paul describes his new direction, it is never as from one faith to another, what we typically might call a conversion. Rather, Paul presents it as a new calling within the same faith. As illustrated in this passage from Galatians, he believes that God has given him a new assignment: to preach to non-Jewish believers and fully welcome them as part of the church without requiring them to pass through the standard points that his faith would usually require.[1]

Unfortunately for Paul, not everyone was immediately onboard with his calling. As he mentions in Galatians 1, he did not confer with other apostles of the early church, but instead immediately set about his mission. Eventually, however, he did travel to meet with them, and it could have gone better:

> Then after fourteen years I went up again to Jerusalem with Barnabas, taking Titus along with me. I went up in response to a revelation. Then I laid before them (though only in a private meeting with the acknowledged leaders) the gospel that I proclaim among the Gentiles, in order to make sure that I was not running, or had not run, in vain. But even Titus, who was with me, was not compelled to be circumcised, though he was a Greek. But because of false believers secretly brought in, who slipped in to spy on the freedom we have in Christ Jesus, so that they might enslave us—we did not submit to them even for a moment, so that the truth of the gospel might always remain with you. And from those who were supposed to be acknowledged leaders (what they actually were makes no difference to me; God shows no partiality)—those leaders contributed nothing to me. On the contrary, when they saw that I had been entrusted with the gospel for the uncircumcised, just as Peter had been entrusted with the gospel for the circumcised (for

---

1. Stendahl, *Paul Among Jews and Gentiles*, 7.

> he who worked through Peter making him an apostle to
> the circumcised also worked through me in sending me
> to the Gentiles), and when James and Cephas and John,
> who were acknowledged pillars, recognized the grace
> that had been given to me, they gave to Barnabas and me
> the right hand of fellowship, agreeing that we should go
> to the Gentiles and they to the circumcised. They asked
> only one thing, that we remember the poor, which was
> actually what I was eager to do. (Galatians 2:1–10)

Jerusalem was a headquarters of sorts for the Jesus Movement, with notable leaders such as Peter, James, and John among those who would have been there for this meeting. Paul says that he finally acquiesced to such a meeting after having a revelation of his own to do so. This, along with what he says later about the other apostles' authority ("what they actually were makes no difference . . . God shows no partiality"), suggests that he may have been content to continue with his own sense of calling and ministry, but wanted to achieve some semblance of endorsement and unity with the larger movement.

Contrast this with those whom he calls "false believers," who were also present, likely a group arguing for the full conversion of Gentiles via circumcision, who were bringing accusations against him. Paul had no interest in their approval, although they were making trouble for him nonetheless. Any challenges or complications to his being seen as an authority among the other apostles necessitated this meeting. Whatever he could do to eliminate some of the questions about his apostleship to the Gentiles, he was glad to do it.

In Galatians as a whole, a large issue for his writing is again to push back against what was contrary to his proclamation. Recounting this meeting was one way of easing any concerns about this, and to show that his message is fully in line with and accepted by the apostles in Jerusalem. They could have limited or prevented this, insisting instead on a more unified or regulated approach according to what they'd already established, but instead recognized the movement of God in Paul's life and the importance of his work to their larger mission.

And so near the end of this passage he notes that Peter, James, and John—whom he is sure to name-drop as "acknowledged pillars"—recognized the grace of God at work in his ministry and agreed to his extension of what they were already doing in other pockets of people around the larger region. Hopefully this would help shore up any doubts that the Galatians had, given the potential influence of other competing messages trying to discredit Paul's standing among them.

The book of Acts mentions that Paul's trade was tentmaking. In Acts 18, he meets two fellow members of his trade, named Priscilla (sometimes Prisca) and Aquila, and the three of them work alongside each other both in their business and in their proclaiming of the gospel. Paul also mentions this couple as beloved friends and coworkers in his letter to the Romans, an important byproduct first established by his plying his trade.

This would also have allowed Paul to move around from city to city to set up shop during working hours, and then proclaim and debate his message about Jesus in the public square when he was finished for the day. At least at the beginning of his ministry, Paul's business provided an entry point for his larger calling.

Paul also alludes to his trade in 1 Thessalonians 2:9, where he reminds them of the labor he undertook while he was with them: "we worked night and day, so that we might not burden any of you while we proclaimed to you the gospel of God." Paul's making of tents provided a context for his ministry, but also very much his livelihood. In 1 Thessalonians, he was very concerned with not wanting to burden this community with an extra stretching of their resources, so he earned his own way instead.

The other part of the strategy of Paul and others toward proclaiming their message about Jesus would have been the conversion of entire households. In numerous places in his letters, Paul refers to the heads of households or to the church within a person's house, showing that the home was an early core building block for the Jesus Movement. In 1 Corinthians 1, Paul mentions Chloe's "people," who would have been members of her house, as well as baptizing the household of Stephanas. In Romans 16, he sends greetings to the households of Aristobulus and Narcissus, among other believers. In Philippians 4:22, he mentions the household of Caesar. The letter to Philemon includes a greeting to the church in his house in verse 2.

The house would not just have been the basic family unit, as we are accustomed to thinking of it today. It also would have included extended family, slaves, hired workers, and sometimes fellow tradespeople who were staying with them.[2] As the head of the house went, so too would everyone else staying under the roof.

This had numerous implications for the early church. First, it gave its evangelistic mission a certain character and focus, as proclaiming to the head of the house would have an effect on everyone else for whom they were responsible. Second, it helped the early church organize itself and care for one another just by giving an extra dimension and reason for the people already looking after each other to continue doing so in a new way. And finally, it would entail these house churches becoming networked with one another for purposes such as occasional larger gatherings of worship, teaching, and fellowship, and supporting one another as others had need. This was not the only strategy employed by Paul and others, but it was an essential one.

Paul's sense of call to proclaim Jesus to the Gentiles involved quite a bit of travel to different and diverse communities around a large region of the world. It pushed and expanded boundaries that had been set by the establishment. It had a certain renegade aspect to it in the eyes of those who preferred a narrower and more rigid approach and focus. Its organization was more portable, structured by a network of houses and individuals rather than a larger regulatory meeting space that oversaw its members more closely.

For Paul, the church is a living thing, with a nimble quality and many moving parts to it than could possibly be controlled. Its soul was the power and grace of God, which many humans have tried to fence in to their own frustration. But its soul is also the

2. Meeks, *First Urban Christians*, 75–76.

people themselves: those who received the good news about Jesus and would contribute to its ongoing life in the world, allowing it to give its hearers what they need rather than what we'd prefer.

THE CHURCH IS NOT A BUILDING

In his book *Eager to Love*, Richard Rohr explores the faith and life of Francis of Assisi, who among other things had a reputation for his connection to and appreciation of God's creation. As Francis was a monk, the name for his room in the monastery was known as a "cell." Not to be confused with the cell one may picture related to incarceration, this was simply a modest room where one would sleep, pray, read, and write away from community worship, meals, and chores.

Francis saw all of nature as sacred and as a setting in which to experience God's presence. For him, one did not need to be in his cell or even in a church to find a connection to God. In fact, he thought it more likely to find that connection out in the world. Rohr quotes him as saying, "Wherever we are, wherever we go, we bring our cell with us. Our brother body is our cell and our soul is the hermit living in the cell. If our soul does not live in peace and solitude within this cell, of what avail is it to live in a man-made cell?"[3]

Francis invited people to change their concept of encountering God, and one way he did that is by redefining some of the terms by which one considers such things. He changed the definition of a cell from that of a physical room to one's body, in which one's soul resides. Likewise, he changed the definition of a monastery from that of a single building to all of creation. We carry our cell with us at all times within the great cathedral of all that God has made, and thus we are constantly presented with the opportunity to receive what God is trying to share with us through it.

For some, it might be quite a radical notion to move from the traditional definitions of church. For many Christians, the word "church" may call to mind a few different things. First, one may

3. Rohr, *Eager to Love*, 47–48.

use it to describe a Sunday morning worship gathering. When one says they are "going to church," they typically mean an event held at a certain time of the week where one may sing, pray, and hear a sermon. This leads us to the second image of church that may come to mind for many, that being a particular building to which one travels to experience this event and others related to the life of a congregation that meets there.

Activities and buildings like these carry with them the possibility of impactful experiences and hold deep meaning for millions of people. But in addition to those, Francis invited people to think even bigger: church can be anywhere and happen at any time, because in a sense Christian believers are always carrying it with them.

The TARDIS is an integral part of The Doctor's adventures. It makes traveling to different times and worlds possible, and not much would happen without it. But The Doctor and their companions rarely remain inside it. After all, what fun is it to go to all these interesting and exciting places if they never actually leave the ship to experience them?

And even once they leave the physical TARDIS, they still carry it with them. An ongoing connection to it allows them to understand the beings that they encounter, and sometimes allows them to breathe and be protected, among other abilities. In that sense, The Doctor and others never really leave it behind.

For Paul, the word "church" could have had a number of possible meanings. It could have referred to the house in which a particular converted family resided, but it also could have meant the extended network of groups and individuals that spanned an entire city. He used it to refer to communities of various sizes, and communities within communities. For Paul, churches ebbed and flowed, expanded and contracted, and moved about the populace whether together for worship and prayer or scattered in daily work or the tasks of service and evangelism.

Both Paul and The Doctor were travelers, going from place to place to check in on or help people as best they could. For either of them, to stay in one spot was to be less effective than they'd like.

Their visions were of a larger world or universe that needed what they could give, even beyond the preferences of those who wanted them to submit to more structure and regulation. The Doctor saw Time Lord technology as holding great potential to do good for others and had to defy his superiors to do it. Paul had a personal experience of God that directed him outside the specified bounds of the Jesus Movement to expand its reach, first to the Jerusalem leaders' chagrin and then to their acceptance.

Many may be so used to thinking about the church as being an activity or a place. One may tend to think of it as having walls, either in the physical sense of a structure with a steeple and stained glass, or in the sense of having defined criteria for who gets to be part of it and who doesn't. One may prefer these walls because they enjoy participating in keeping them raised against a world that they want to repel. Many others have experienced what it's like to have a wall placed in their path as they are denied inclusion and acceptance.

The Doctor and Paul see the pitfalls of such walls and actively explore a calling to make them much more permeable. A TARDIS is for traveling, and for leaving in order to see to others' needs. A church is for inviting more people in to find hope and healing, and for easing burdens rather than adding to them. They are both for active use for the benefit of others, rather than keeping to oneself.

As Francis suggests, our view of how God is present in the world and especially in the lives of hurting people changes when we consider that all the universe is God's dwelling place. God calls us out of our boxes and buildings to experience the bigger, richer, deeper possibilities for a divine encounter all around. Such boxes and buildings may hold a sacred significance, but we carry that same sacredness at all times, wherever we go.

3

The Struggle with Identity

"INTO THE DALEK" is the second episode after The Doctor has regenerated into his twelfth form. At the very beginning of this episode, he and his companion Clara are together on the TARDIS, and he invites her to sit down next to him. At this point, he says that he needs the truth from her. After she agrees, he asks her, "Am I a good man?"

The question that The Doctor asks is not often this bluntly put, but there are other times over the course of the show where the struggle over their purpose and identity is central to how events play out for them and for those they're trying to help. The Doctor learns and grows and wrestles with who they want to be for others and for the universe, and the answers to the question are not always positive or affirming, giving cause for self-reflection. Viewers, fans, and many of the show's characters may celebrate many of The Doctor's heroic actions, but there have come times for The Doctor that have brought pause and self-realization regarding their motivations as well.

One instance where this is the case spans two episodes called "The Fires of Pompeii" and "The Waters of Mars," both during the tenure of The Tenth Doctor. During the former, The Doctor and his companion Donna find themselves in the prosperous city of Pompeii, the day before Vesuvius erupts. Upon this realization,

Donna immediately wants to find ways to warn everyone to evacu-ate, but The Doctor insists that the events to come are fixed in time and cannot be altered. He would rather the two of them just leave before things are put in motion.

Unfortunately for them, the TARDIS is placed in the home of an art dealer (played by Peter Capaldi years before he'd become The Doctor himself), and the two get to know him, his family, and some of the strange happenings around the city. This eventually leads them to the discovery of an alien spaceship at the heart of Vesuvius, which is the true cause of the earthquakes that the area is experiencing. At this point, The Doctor discovers that the only way to thwart their plot involves getting the mountain to erupt, which also causes him to realize that he is the one who destroys the city.

As the lava and fire begin to descend upon Pompeii, Donna again begs The Doctor to at least save the family they've befriend-ed, to which he reluctantly agrees. Yet the fact that he was the cause of everyone's suffering to begin with lingers.

Later in the same season, The Tenth Doctor has parted ways with Donna and finds himself on the first human-made base on Mars. He meets the captain, whose name helps him recall that this base becomes famous because it is blown up for unknown reasons, and the crew memorialized. As with Pompeii, The Doctor insists that he has to leave quickly before events set in motion, but he again becomes involved before he can do so.

The great discovery here is that a virus is overtaking the crew one by one through the water supply. The captain sets evacuation procedures in motion but also insists that The Doctor tell her what happens to them. He shares that the captain ends up pushing the button to destroy the base so that the virus can't get to Earth. And yet her death inspires many, including her granddaughter, to push further out into space to explore and create new possibilities. "Your death creates the future," he says. That's why he can't help, especially after what happened at Pompeii.

As The Doctor makes his way to the TARDIS, he can hear the remaining crew struggling to fend off their infected colleagues. He listens long enough and is moved to turn back to save them. At this point, the captain objects after all she's been told, pulling them into the TARDIS and escaping to Earth.

As they exit the TARDIS, the three remaining crew members are baffled and frightened. The Doctor asks simply, "Isn't anyone going to thank me?" He boasts of being a victorious Time Lord who saves the little people, marveling at how good he is and how nothing is impossible for him now. The captain is aghast, wondering what will become of her granddaughter's inspiration, as well as the future of Earth, leading her to go into her house and kill herself, which resets original developments to where they need to be.

It is only after he hears what the captain has done that The Doctor comes to himself and realizes how much he overstepped in saving her. He'd only been fueled by ego and selfishness rather than a desire to help; a need to overcompensate for a previous perceived failure when it wasn't his place to do so.

One of the ever-present stories hinted at throughout *Doctor Who* since its 2005 revival is the events of the Time War, a great war between the Time Lords and Daleks that ended after The Doctor blew up Gallifrey. Ever since, The Doctor has been carrying around a great deal of sorrow and regret for what he felt was necessary in order to make the fighting stop.

This regret has been so deep, in fact, that The Doctor has even suppressed all memory of the past self who did it, whom we finally meet at the end of "The Name of the Doctor." Played by John Hurt, this iteration isn't even allowed to go by the name The Doctor because his actions broke the promise of the name to heal and to help. Yet this past self insists that he did what he did in the name of peace and sanity.

We see more of this past Doctor—usually called the War Doctor in lieu of a traditional number—in the fiftieth anniversary special, "The Day of the Doctor." Near the end of the Time War, we see the War Doctor steal the powerful bomb that he'll use to destroy Gallifrey, a bomb so powerful, in fact, that we're told it has developed a conscience. This conscience takes the form of past companion Rose Tyler, who transports him to meet his future selves who have to carry around the weight of his decision.

The War Doctor ends up meeting both The Tenth and Eleventh Doctors, who share their resentment of him and of their own actions. Among other things, the three have a conversation about how many they realize they killed the day they set off the bomb. The War Doctor even wonders how many worlds his future regret has saved; how much more inspired and driven he becomes to save others. "You were The Doctor on the day it was impossible to get it right," The Eleventh Doctor eventually comments to his earlier self. It is a comment that may not bring much relief, but at least acknowledges something of the complexity of the War Doctor's decision.

After an entire season of wrestling with the question, "Am I a good man?," The Twelfth Doctor comes face to face with his old nemesis, The Master, now in the form of Missy. She presents him with control of a vast Cyberman army that he can use to battle all threats to the universe. She tries to argue that the two of them are not so different, but The Doctor strongly disagrees, finally realizing the answer to his own question: "I am not a good man, and I am not a bad man . . . I am an idiot with a box and a screwdriver passing through, helping out, learning."

In this latest instance, The Doctor learns to think much less of himself than in other times when thinking too highly came with a great cost. He learns to acknowledge his limitations and his reliance on others, a lesson that previously has not often come before grave mistakes and dire consequences.

The Doctor will still prove to be imperfect and flawed after this revelation, and will continue to learn the limits of his or her own knowledge and reasoning. When The Doctor has chosen to ignore such limitations, as with "The Fires of Pompeii" and "The Waters of Mars," the price has been steep. At other times, as during the Time War, The Doctor acts on what he sees as the best course even if it is still one of the worst, and has to live with the aftermath hoping to make up for it down the road.

The Doctor asking "Am I a good person?" is an important exercise in self-awareness, illustrating the struggle to act in ways concurrent with what someone who has chosen a name representing healing, life, and helping others. The Doctor has not always gotten it right, but to their credit knows it, and tries to do better the next time.

Even so, what are the implications of such a struggle with identity? How can realizing our limitations help us deepen our own sense of self?

THE LEAST OF THE APOSTLES

Paul's original purpose in his letters was to instruct, encourage, and correct the faith communities with which he was in relationship. Interwoven into these letters are references to his own self-understanding and struggles with identity. Sometimes this is to acknowledge or add clarity to how these communities may view him and consequently receive his ministry. At other times he uses himself as an example from which to learn.

When he writes to the Philippians, for instance, he is engaging in a debate common between himself and others in that time, that being on the subject of circumcision:

> Finally, my brothers and sisters, rejoice in the Lord. To write the same things to you is not troublesome to me, and for you it is a safeguard. Beware of the dogs, beware of the evil workers, beware of those who mutilate the flesh! For it is we who are the circumcision, who worship in the Spirit of God and boast in Christ Jesus and have no confidence in the flesh—even though I, too, have reason for confidence in the flesh. If anyone else has reason to be confident in the flesh, I have more: circumcised on the eighth day, a member of the people of Israel, of the tribe of Benjamin, a Hebrew born of Hebrews; as to the law, a Pharisee; as to zeal, a persecutor of the church; as to righteousness under the law, blameless. Yet whatever gains I had, these I have come to regard as loss because of Christ. More than that, I regard everything as loss because of the

surpassing value of knowing Christ Jesus my Lord. For
his sake I have suffered the loss of all things, and I regard
them as rubbish, in order that I may gain Christ and be
found in him, not having a righteousness of my own that
comes from the law, but one that comes through faith
in Christ, the righteousness from God based on faith. I
want to know Christ and the power of his resurrection
and the sharing of his sufferings by becoming like him in
his death, if somehow I may attain the resurrection from
the dead. (Philippians 3:1–11)

Paul's primary intention in this part of the letter is to warn
the Philippian community about a group of people who seem to be
preaching a very different message than what Paul has presented.
This message hinges on the importance of becoming circumcised
as being a proper symbolic action of faithful relationship with
God. The language that Paul uses suggests that the presence of this
other group has evoked a strong reaction, as he calls them "dogs"
and "evil workers," and "mutilators of the flesh."

Why might he choose terms like these? It may be less to
indict this other group in the eyes of the Philippians—although
such names certainly would do that—and more to keep the group
focused on what he has presented to them instead. A message
leaning on outward physical alteration involves "confidence in the
flesh," a phrase he will soon use to make his counterpoint. It takes
more than a ritual action by human effort to achieve God's favor.
And, in fact, human effort is not actually a factor at all.

This becomes clearer in the following verses, when Paul
presents a sort of mini-resume. He lists some of the highlights of
his own achievements to illustrate just how much confidence in
the flesh he could have, if gaining God's approval relied on such
things. He was circumcised when he was eight days old, as Jews
raised from birth would have been. He was a full-born member of
the people of Israel. He was well trained in the law and faithfully
kept it as a Pharisee. He even lists his former days of persecuting
his fellow Christian believers as an illustration of his dedication to
the tradition. Paul is an Apostle Victorious when it comes to being

able to lift up his accomplishments to God, if that's what it takes to earn points in the heavenly ledger.

The real point that Paul wants to make in listing these, however, is not to one-up this other group, nor to impress the Philippians. He actually does it to discredit the argument that God's favor depends on human effort. All that he has done doesn't matter as much as receiving God's grace offered in Christ. He will dump every trophy that he has earned in the trash because knowing Christ is the more important thing. He would rather the Philippians take on such an attitude as well, seeking to receive God's freely offered gifts in gratitude and living in faithful response to it instead.

While presenting himself to the Philippians may have gone over well as an illustration, he tells of an internal struggle with which he wrestles in his letter to the Romans that doesn't present him in such a positive light:

> I do not understand my own actions. For I do not do what I want, but I do the very thing I hate. Now if I do what I do not want, I agree that the law is good. But in fact it is no longer I that do it, but sin that dwells within me. For I know that nothing good dwells within me, that is, in my flesh. I can will what is right, but I cannot do it. For I do not do the good I want, but the evil I do not want is what I do. Now if I do what I do not want, it is no longer I that do it, but sin that dwells within me. (Romans 7:15–20)

This comes as part of a larger discussion that Paul is having about the Mosaic law not being sufficient for addressing sinful behavior. In order to illustrate one's need for something more, he personalizes the predicament of humanity for himself, using his own struggle as an example.

The beginning of this internal conflict is that Paul wants to do good. He knows on an intellectual level what he should do, and so he would like to set out to do it. His chief source of knowledge of the right thing to do comes from the law, but it could also come from what he has observed or has been taught by listening to or watching those whom he considers moral exemplars and teachers.

In any case, his desire to do good is not sufficient, because there is also another desire within him that is working against it. He names it as the indwelling power of sin, which causes him to act against what he knows is right. As he says elsewhere in his letters, humanity is under the power of sin and unable to break from it. This is no different for Paul, as he describes his propensity to do what he doesn't want to do rather than what he'd rather do.

"I can will what is right, but I cannot do it" (7:18). Paul finds himself susceptible to what he knows he shouldn't do, which he names as the power of sin in his life. He knows what he is supposed to do, but he succumbs to temptation to do what he shouldn't do instead.

We could call this Paul's own way of answering The Doctor's earlier question for himself: "Am I a good man?" For Paul, the answer is no, because he needs more than his own willpower to do the good that he knows that he should do.

This is one of several times when Paul is quite honest and vulnerable in his letters about his afflictions and weaknesses. As much as he talks himself up in some instances, he also readily admits his own frailty. As he has noted his own sinfulness in Romans 7, he also talks about his own weakness in 2 Corinthians:

> It is necessary to boast; nothing is to be gained by it, but I will go on to visions and revelations of the Lord. I know a person in Christ who fourteen years ago was caught up to the third heaven—whether in the body or out of the body I do not know; God knows. And I know that such a person—whether in the body or out of the body I do not know; God knows—was caught up into Paradise and heard things that are not to be told, that no mortal is permitted to repeat. On behalf of such a one I will boast, but on my own behalf I will not boast, except of my weaknesses. But if I wish to boast, I will not be a fool, for I will be speaking the truth. But I refrain from it, so that no one may think better of me than what is seen in me or heard from me, even considering the exceptional character of the revelations. Therefore, to keep me from being too elated, a thorn was given me in the flesh, a messenger of

Satan to torment me, to keep me from being too elated. Three times I appealed to the Lord about this, that it would leave me, but he said to me, "My grace is sufficient for you, for power is made perfect in weakness." So, I will boast all the more gladly of my weaknesses, so that the power of Christ may dwell in me. Therefore I am content with weaknesses, insults, hardships, persecutions, and calamities for the sake of Christ; for whenever I am weak, then I am strong. (2 Corinthians 12:1–10)

There are two parts to this passage. In the first, Paul recounts a vision that he had of being taken up to a heavenly realm. He makes some effort to distance himself from it by speaking of himself in the third person, though his success in this is up for debate. He also doesn't know whether he was taken out of his body for the experience and is unable to repeat what he heard or saw while there. Nevertheless, he says, he has cause to boast as a result of receiving such a vision, and could do so, given that once again he is dealing with opponents to his ministry in this community, who may have been less modest in their own boasting about visions to boost their status and lessen his.[1]

In this passage, Paul is more interested in using his vision as a setup not to boast but to talk about an unnamed affliction that he is trying to keep in check. He notes a "thorn in the flesh" that had been given to him to torment him and keep him humble. Many have speculated as to what this could have been, and theories range from epilepsy to malaria to migraines to seizures to depression to bipolar disorder.[2]

The nature of the ailment may be less important than its effects on Paul's spiritual self-understanding, at least for the purposes of why he mentions it. While he could rest on the laurels of something like the visions he has had or the credentials that he has amassed over the course of his life, he instead finds those opportunities tempered by his own weaknesses, which says he has begged God to remove from his life but have remained.

1. Sampley, "Second Letter to the Corinthians," 162.
2. Roetzel, *2 Corinthians*, 111.

Rather than lament this weakness, Paul instead names how it has made him more dependent upon God's power to carry him onward in his mission and life. Where his own ability to boast decreases, his ability to rest in God's ability to continue working through him may only grow. Such limitations may help him refrain from overstepping in his own ability and authority. And rather than see himself as a good man or a bad man, by the grace of God he's just an idiot with a message for the Gentiles, passing through, helping out, sharing God's love, and learning.

THE PROCESS OF DISCOVERY

In many episodes of *Doctor Who*, we see The Doctor learn more about themselves as it happens. "The Fires of Pompeii" and "The Waters of Mars" show an arc of The Doctor discovering that he is responsible for a massive historical tragedy, and the former episode explores his reactions to and learning from the events of that episode. He copes with the imperfect solution of losing millions of lives to save billions, but also allows Donna to convince him to at least save a few people from what he's helped set in motion.

He carries these events into the latter episode, where at first he tries to overcompensate in one direction by trying to remove himself as much as possible from what happens to the crew on the Mars base. As he becomes more involved, however, the pendulum swings so far in the opposite direction that he decides he will never allow lives to be lost again, because he is so confident in his abilities and in his sense of call as hero to the universe. By the end, he further discovers that this is not the empirically correct response either, and again must wrestle with feelings of regret and carry the lesson into future adventures.

It is more interesting for the viewer to see this process of discovery. Part of what makes The Doctor a compelling character is how they react and learn from the scenarios placed in their path, not only for the benefit of those they are trying to help, but also in how successes and failures influence them from beginning to end, and sometimes beyond. The Doctor's own struggles are an active part of the story.

When we read Paul's letters, he is able to edit out much of the messiness that has led to his conclusions. We are not often privy to what led him to decide that all his accomplishments don't mean nearly as much as knowing Christ and proclaiming God's grace for Gentiles. What sort of a thought process finally helped him conclude this? Was it a single moment, or did it involve long sleepless nights of reflection, prayer, and humility?

Likewise, when Paul writes about his unnamed "thorn in the flesh," what were those times of begging God to remove it from him look like? Did the prayers that he lifted to God feature contrite words of piety that would have made King James jealous, or did they sound more like Robert Duvall in *The Apostle*, yelling at God late into the evening wanting to be rid of this source of suffering?

Paul's letters contain much less of the process and he instead shares his conclusions, which will be much more instructive to his communities anyway. He is more concerned with helping them stay on a faithful path, and delving too much into his own struggles would distract from that. So he offers just enough to serve the point that he wants to make, without dwelling on them.

As a result, we see what Paul has become much more than how he got there. His struggles were likely no less difficult and provided no less regret, second-guessing, mistakes, and false starts, but he is reluctant to pull back the curtain too much for the sake of his audience. He is, however, willing to share some of his imperfection with them, to remind them that the life of faith does not come without occasionally wrestling with God and oneself to deepen one's understanding of both.

The people whom we most admire—spiritual leaders, musicians, speakers, writers, performers, athletes, mentors—did not achieve their level of competency and wisdom without their own processes of struggle and self-discovery. While the age of the Internet and social media has made more of their lives in between accomplishments and completed projects accessible, we are often privy to only a small portion of the frustrations, disappointments, and breakthroughs that helped get them to that point.

The Doctor and Paul both show that any process of discovery, whether figuring out one's own place in the world or asking specifically about the presence and influence of God on that potential place, does not follow a single, straightforward trajectory. Rather, it includes affirmations on mountaintops, uncertainty in dark valleys, detours, U-turns, trying the same path a second or third time, and the full range of emotions that we may feel in reaction to any of it.

But The Doctor and Paul also both show us that the process is not for standing still. Rather, it is for traveling. It will not be the hero's journey that we imagine or hope for. Instead, it will show us who we really are, which is what we need.

4

Strength in What Seems Weak

IN OVER FIFTY YEARS' worth of episodes, The Doctor has saved individuals, planets, or the universe countless times. Yet it is worth noting that the methods The Doctor uses rarely involve violence or coercion as a first resort. Instead, they often investigate or explore the causes for a conflict, the resources at hand, and attempt to appeal to the better nature of the sides involved. The Doctor does not carry a weapon, but instead a sonic screwdriver, which suggests that their primary drive is repairing or healing (as someone named The Doctor would have), rather than storming in and blasting others like so many other on-screen heroes do.

The Doctor is sometimes criticized for this approach, as some would rather they act in what they deem more conventional ways: using force rather than reason, and destruction rather than compassion. The Doctor's enemies—and sometimes their friends—see their non-violent ways as too weak to be much good.

This is no better portrayed than when The Doctor runs into the most notorious monsters in the show's universe, the Daleks. These enemies of the Time Lord have been around since The Doctor's first incarnation, always causing major trouble for the characters. Their appearance is like a robot on wheels, with a suction cup for grabbing or manipulating objects, and a very powerful laser blaster. They see with a single protruding visualizer on their domed heads. Their speech is also robotic, as there is not much variation in their inflection. All of this belies the fact that these large and dangerous structures are actually casings for a fragile form inside that drives the outer part like a tank.

We first see how these creatures are developed in "Genesis of the Daleks," where The Fourth Doctor is sent to the planet Skaro at the very beginning of the Daleks' development. At this point, the planet is beset by an ongoing war between two groups, the Thals and the Kaleds. The Kaleds are depending on a genius named Davros to develop a new method of defeating their longtime enemies.

"Genesis of the Daleks" is Davros's first appearance, although he becomes a recurring character and one of The Doctor's primary enemies. He is disabled, seated in a wheelchair reminiscent of the lower part of the Daleks' metal form. He also has a robotic eye in the center of his forehead that replaces his biological eyes, also reminiscent of the Daleks' single sight mechanism. In this series, The Doctor describes Davros as a genius with a fanatical desire to perpetuate himself through his new creations. The Doctor also notes that he works without conscience or pity.

The Daleks' biological programming reflects Davros's mentality. He strives to take away their sense of pity and their discernment of right and wrong. When he begins to tweak his first prototype Daleks to remove these pieces of their mental makeup, he refers to it as making an improvement. Calling conscience an "affliction," Davros does all he can to eliminate it from his creations' psyches, so that only their desire to dominate through force and extermination remains.

We gain quite a bit of knowledge about Davros's philosophy in this series, as well as what he intends for the Daleks to do and how he intends for them to act. He sees their dominance through threats and destruction as the best way to bring peace to his planet and to the entire universe. In contrast, he calls democracy, freedom, and fairness "the creed of cowards," seeing victory as being achieved through power and strength rather than reconciliation or empathy. No race can survive without aggression, he argues, and his goal is to have the Daleks motivated as purely by aggression as he can achieve. Through this, he reasons, they will become the most dominant force in the universe. This mindest is displayed by the Daleks in every episode or series in which they appear.

Things have changed quite a bit by the time The Ninth Doctor has his first meeting with a Dalek. His incarnation comes after the Time War between the Time Lords and Daleks, where he orchestrated the destruction of both races in order to stop the conflict. In "Dalek," he lands in a deep underground bunker and laboratory run by a man named Henry Van Statton, who has captured the one remaining Dalek in the entire universe.

When The Doctor comes face to face with his enemy, his first instinct is to rage at it. His foe has been greatly weakened and is incapable of fighting, leading The Doctor to ask, "If you can't kill, what's the point of you?" When asked to describe what the Dalek is to those who have discovered it, including his companion Rose, The Doctor recalls its stated objective to kill anything different, and actually uses the term "racial cleansing," which was alluded to back in "Genesis of the Daleks." Every single emotion, The Doctor says, has been removed except hate. Davros saw this as the superior emotion through which dominance could be achieved.

The Dalek is revived when Rose unwittingly touches it, allowing it to absorb not only her energy but her DNA in order to re-energize itself. Unfortunately for the Dalek, this makes it part human, causing it to feel fear and empathy and making it hesitant to kill others. Much like when The Doctor asks earlier in the episode, the Dalek asks itself what defines it if it doesn't kill, and it ends up destroying itself because it can conceive of no alternative purpose.

Davros again appears in the two-part episodes of "The Magician's Apprentice" and "The Witch's Familiar," where he calls upon The Twelfth Doctor for help as he sits near the end of his life on Skaro. We first see Davros as a boy caught in the middle of the war between the Thals and Kaleds. The Doctor arrives to help, but changes his mind once he realizes whom the boy is and leaves. Davros remembers this encounter and reminds The Doctor during their latest meeting.

At this point, The Doctor begins to wonder if, by abandoning Davros so long ago, he was the one who inadvertently helped create The Daleks. He ponders the question: "If Davros created the Daleks, who created Davros?" Later, as the two converse, The Doctor also wonders why he keeps letting Davros live, to which Davros responds, "Compassion. It has always been your greatest indulgence." Davros still decries The Doctor's compassion as a weakness, over and against his creations' reliance on hatred and aggression.

After finally escaping what turns out to be a trap set by Davros and the Daleks, The Doctor again travels back to the boy caught in the midst of war in order to save him and introduce mercy and perhaps help deflect the creation of such a malevolent force in the universe.

Throughout their encounters with the Daleks, and particularly Davros, The Doctor persists in the belief that non-violent means will yet defeat a species of creatures that sees such tactics as weakness and favors brutality as the means to victory instead.

In "The Witch's Familiar," Davros comments to The Doctor, "Compassion grows in you like a cancer," to which he responds, "I hope so." Such is the nature of the conflict between the two.

PAUL'S WEAKNESS, GOD'S COMFORT

The first letter to the Corinthians is one of Paul's more confrontational letters. This faith community had a number of problems, divisions, conflicts, and misunderstandings that Paul does his best to address, one after another.

At the beginning of his letter, he seems to think it best to deal with their struggle to maintain unity with one another.

> Now I appeal to you, brothers and sisters, by the name of our Lord Jesus Christ, that all of you be in agreement and that there be no divisions among you, but that you be united in the same mind and the same purpose. For it has been reported to me by Chloe's people that there are quarrels among you, my brothers and sisters. What I mean

is that each of you says, "I belong to Paul," or "I belong to Apollos," or "I belong to Cephas," or "I belong to Christ." Has Christ been divided? Was Paul crucified for you? Or were you baptized in the name of Paul? I thank God that I baptized none of you except Crispus and Gaius, so that no one can say that you were baptized in my name. (I did baptize also the household of Stephanas; beyond that, I do not know whether I baptized anyone else.)

For Christ did not send me to baptize but to pro-claim the gospel, and not with eloquent wisdom, so that the cross of Christ might not be emptied of its power. (1 Corinthians 1:10–17)

In the earliest years of the Jesus Movement, Paul was far from the only apostle making his way around to different communities to preach, teach, model, and lead. This sending began with the men and women who were direct followers, friends, and students of Jesus, and then Paul and others began as second-generation apostles, working alongside them and continuing this work of sup-porting faith communities across the region.

This part of the letter mentions Cephas, better known to many as Peter, and another figure named Apollos. Paul uses their names to make a point about divisions based on loyalty to a particular apostle. The chief issue seems to be that some feel a special affinity to certain people based on who baptized them. Peter was not really a known entity among the Corinthians as much as the other two apostles mentioned, so the real source of the conflict would have been more between people pledging loyalty to Paul or Apollos.[1]

Such divisions based on favorites is likely a familiar concept to most. Those who have been part of a church could perhaps name clergy whose style of preaching, teaching, or other skills that they preferred over and against those who came before or after them. Fans of *Doctor Who* have had many a long conversa-tion—sometimes friendly, sometimes less so—about which actor or actress to play The Doctor has been their favorite, for reasons ranging from how they looked to how they behaved to how they dressed, and so on.

1. Horsley, *1 Corinthians*, 45.

For various reasons, the Corinthian believers are drawing similar distinctions based on preferences, and Paul is seeing that the community as a whole is suffering because of it. So he is taking the time to remind them that it is not a certain apostle or preacher or teacher whom they are meant to follow, but Christ. And likewise, this single Christ who was crucified and raised is the point of unity for all disciples everywhere, regardless of who baptized you.

At the very end of this passage, Paul hints at what may have been one cause for people preferring the ministry of other apostles over his own when he says that Christ did not send him to proclaim "with eloquent words of wisdom" (1:17). People in that time and place would have made a close association between how well-spoken someone was and the amount of wisdom that they had. Greek and Hellenistic culture greatly valued the discussion of ideas in public spaces, and eloquent speech was often a sign of education, status, and knowledge.[2]

Paul, however, states that he did not come proclaiming with eloquence or wisdom. He may have struggled with public speaking for one reason or another. More than once in his letters, he hints at physical ailments that limited him in different ways and may have diminished how some viewed him as a result. They might have preferred more conventionally well-spoken and wise teachers who looked and sounded the part more than he did.[3]

In other words, to some Paul seemed weak, while others seemed strong, by traditional societal standards. For that reason, what Paul writes next about the cross has a personal dimension for him as well as a larger purpose for Christian unity.

> For the message about the cross is foolishness to those who are perishing, but to us who are being saved it is the power of God. For it is written, "I will destroy the wisdom of the wise, and the discernment of the discerning I will thwart." Where is the one who is wise? Where is the scribe? Where is the debater of this age? Has not God made foolish the wisdom of the world? For since, in the wisdom of God, the

2. Horsley, *1 Corinthians*, 46–47.

3. Stendahl, *Paul Among Jews and Gentiles*, 43.

world did not know God through wisdom, God decided, through the foolishness of our proclamation, to save those who believe. For Jews demand signs and Greeks desire wisdom, but we proclaim Christ crucified, a stumbling block to Jews and foolishness to Gentiles, but to those who are the called, both Jews and Greeks, Christ the power of God and the wisdom of God. For God's foolishness is wiser than human wisdom, and God's weakness is stronger than human strength. Consider your own call, brothers and sisters: not many of you were wise by human standards, not many were powerful, not many were of noble birth. But God chose what is foolish in the world to shame the wise; God chose what is weak in the world to shame the strong; God chose what is low and despised in the world, things that are not, to reduce to nothing things that are, so that no one might boast in the presence of God. He is the source of your life in Christ Jesus, who became for us wisdom from God, and righteousness and sanctification and redemption, in order that, as it is written, "Let the one who boasts, boast in the Lord." (1 Corinthians 1:18–31)

In verse 17, Paul contrasts the cross of Christ over and against eloquent words of wisdom.[4] This sets the table for the subsequent passage, where he expounds upon why he does so, beyond making the case for his own ministry and apostleship.

Quite simply, he says, the cross seems like a foolish thing to offer to the world as good news. It was a symbol of humiliation, failure, and death. Crucifixion was an extreme form of capital punishment for lower-class criminals to help keep the population in check. People who were crucified hung as examples to others not to defy the great Roman Empire, lest the same fate await them as well.[5]

Messiahs didn't die, let alone in a manner so degrading as crucifixion. To preach about the crucified Jesus as the revelation and source of God's saving power would have been laughable. Jesus couldn't have been strong; the people who killed him and

4. Sampley, "First Letter to the Corinthians," 808.
5. Horsley, *1 Corinthians*, 50.

left him as a bloody example for the rest of the movement he was inspiring had true strength. He was merely another of countless victims squashed by the ones who had true power.

This is why, throughout this passage, Paul admits that the message of the cross seems so foolish and weak. By all traditional measures, talking about the crucified Jesus would have seemed ridiculous. If he was truly powerful, he would have displayed some countermove to overtake his oppressors. If he was truly wise, he would have either avoided the cross or found a way to get out of it.

And yet Paul persists, as he suggests that the cross overturns our typical ideas of what true power and wisdom is. After all, God had more of the story to tell after Jesus' death. God raised Jesus, rendering earthly displays of power impotent. Through the resurrection, God shows the usual conceptions of strength to be weak, and the usual qualities of wisdom to be foolish. Those who crucified Jesus thought they knew best, and then God showed them that they didn't know anything.

"God made foolish the wisdom of the world," Paul writes. The wisdom of this world, with its emphases on authority through strength and peace through elimination, stands in opposition to what God reveals through the cross and resurrection.[6] It is the same argument that plays out between The Doctor and Davros when the former advocates for compassion and mercy while the latter champions domination and extermination.

Paul again alludes to his own struggles and weakness:

> When I came to you, brothers and sisters, I did not come proclaiming the mystery of God to you in lofty words or wisdom. For I decided to know nothing among you except Jesus Christ, and him crucified. And I came to you in weakness and in fear and in much trembling. My speech and my proclamation were not with plausible words of wisdom, but with a demonstration of the Spirit and of power, so that your faith might rest not on human wisdom but on the power of God. (1 Corinthians 2:1–5)

6. Borg and Crossan, *First Paul*, 135.

At the root of Paul's theological reasoning is the personal stake that he has in it, as well as its larger implications for the immediate problem playing out among the Corinthians. Not only does the cross put traditional notions of power and wisdom on notice, but he hopes that the people of this beloved community can see how it applies to them.

Paul came to the Corinthians with his own weaknesses and his own limitations of knowledge and speech. It was by the Spirit that he proclaimed to them and served among them faithfully. He appeals to them to remember, and to see the deeper power of God at work through him just as it has been through the cross. He urges them to rally around the unexpected, strange, foolish-looking ways that God is working in the world, rather than the usual showings of power that may look or sound good but work in contrast with what God does through the cross of Christ.

WHAT IS STRONG VS. WHAT IS EASY

Both The Doctor and Paul strive to help others see a different way of evaluating strength and wisdom, and they each struggle to convince others of the alternative possibilities.

While The Doctor does not always succeed in showing compassion toward his archenemies, the Daleks, he nevertheless attempts to do so in several cases, particularly with Davros. In part due to his only knowing war in his developmental days and later his charge to come up with a way to defeat the Kaleds' enemies, Davros always insists that things like love, kindness, and sympathy are weaknesses. He and the Daleks only see the universe in terms of winning and losing, of domination or being dominated. And so they conclude that the only way to exist is to exterminate all those whom they see as lesser beings because they are not able to fight back.

On more than one occasion, The Doctor tries to give the Daleks the benefit of the doubt that they can change. There are times when they show signs of progressing forward from their destructive ways, and The Doctor acts in hope that they can know a different way of existing alongside other species.

In the two-part story of "Daleks in Manhattan" and "Evolution of the Daleks," for instance, The Tenth Doctor meets a small remnant of Daleks who are hatching a plot to merge themselves with humans so that their species will endure. After a successful test run, The Doctor rushes to help them continue their work. Unfortunately, when the other Daleks realize that their new merged subject displays a desire to live in peace with others, they kill him and give up their plan. Where The Doctor had hoped for a change in how they categorized strength and weakness, the Daleks resisted it and insisted to remain as they were.

Paul also struggles not only with how believers among the Corinthians see these categories of strength and wisdom, but with how they view him and his ministry. He comes to them in a condition that to some doesn't seem as attractive or engaging or articulate as some other apostles with whom they had a relationship, and something about who he is and how he expresses himself does not hold appeal for them the way others who don't suffer from his ailments do.

Paul's solution is to point the community to the cross and to remind them that God does not think in terms of strength and wisdom the way they do. God does not reward those who are already strong as if they earned something, but instead lifts up and renews those who are weak. God does not only speak through those who are already able to do so at a high level, but instead reveals wisdom through what many may deem foolish.

Both The Doctor and Paul push back against simplistic ways of seeing how the universe works. They challenge the notion that there is only one way to be strong; that only peace may come through victory over someone else. To Davros's dismay, The Doctor protects humanity and others from the Daleks' plots to exterminate them, refusing to accept their mentality that only the strong—that is, only the most aggressive and violent—survive. And Paul takes great pains to show that strength and wisdom are not just in the most popular or charismatic, but in many other forms according to God's turning conventions on their heads through Jesus.

Unfortunately for those who hear The Doctor's and Paul's arguments, these alternatives that they present are more difficult and take greater care and consideration. Dividing the world into stark categories of friend and enemy, worthy and unworthy, those who deserve care and those who deserve punishment, is too easy. This mentality ignores the complexity of existence and of individuals, as well as the possibility of redemption and restoration.

What is true strength? Is it the eradication of all difference; the coercion of someone to the "right" way of life under threat of exclusion or worse? Or might it be, as both The Doctor and Paul show, the more careful consideration of what could happen in the future if even a small amount of kindness or forgiveness were shown today? The former, with its black-and-white thinking and its simple dualistic conception of reality, is much easier: it doesn't require nearly as much thought and it doesn't ask as much of its adherents. The latter, with its blend of hope, mercy, and intention, invites people into a longer and more demanding process of listening, interaction, and entering into another's story.

Paul encourages his hearers and listeners to consider where they started: "not many of you were wise by human standards, not many were powerful, not many were of noble birth. But God chose what is foolish in the world to shame the wise; God chose what is weak in the world to shame the strong" (1 Corinthians 1:26–27). He encourages them to think about where they started and what insights and growth they have experienced since someone began to guide them in love. That intentional showing of regard began to open them to God's calling in their lives. It is not unlike The Doctor choosing to help Davros as a boy, hoping that this small act of rescue may help change his conception of mercy; will help him realize that such actions are strong, even if they aren't as clear-cut.

Time and again, both figures advocate for something more demanding, yet also more rewarding. What seems weak actually requires more strength, and likewise leads to a stronger community, whether in Corinth, Earth, Skaro, or any number of other places in the universe. This approach may seem weak when compared to conventional concepts, but committing to what it asks requires greater wisdom to consider what could be possible, and greater strength to help bring those possibilities into existence.

5

Christ Died for the Pudding Brains

CHARACTERS ON THE SHOW occasionally comment on how much The Doctor seems to love helping the planet Earth over and against other planets. When the Time Lords put The Second Doctor on trial in "The War Games," they observe his affinity for Earth and its people, which is a primary reason for their banishing him there for a while. When The Tenth Doctor meets with an alien species threatening the Earth in "The Christmas Invasion," part of his attempt to dissuade their effort is to argue how much potential human beings have. When Missy offers The Twelfth Doctor a Cyberman army to control in "Death in Heaven," he argues back that he doesn't need an army because he has the expression of love that humanity offers one another to inspire and guide him.

The Doctor is drawn to Earth and to humanity because they seem enamored both with helping them realize who they can be, but also protecting them from the many extraterrestrial forces that also seem fascinated with the notion of conquering or destroying them.

With rare exceptions, most of The Doctor's companions have been human. This is a natural consequence of The Doctor spending so much time in one place and with one species. They are in turn afforded a larger view of the universe beyond their own planet, and The Doctor often takes great joy in watching their fellow travelers marvel, explore, react, and experience the many worlds to which they travel together. The Doctor has a genuine love of opening the minds of human beings, in particular to how much more there is to existence.

All of that is not to say, however, that The Doctor has always thought well of humanity. There have been times throughout the series when The Doctor has become frustrated with or angered by the decisions that humans make, either as individuals or collectively. The Doctor sometimes wonders why they keep helping this planet given some of the ways humans view or treat each other.

In the episode "Father's Day," companion Rose tells The Ninth Doctor the story of how her father was killed by a hit-and-run driver when she was a baby. She includes details such as how there were no witnesses, and nobody to be there with him when he died in the street. She asks The Doctor to take her to that moment so she can see him and act as the witness that her dad never had. The Doctor agrees, and they watch the event unfold.

After this, however, Rose asks if they can go back a second time, which The Doctor is very wary of. Nevertheless, he agrees, and this time Rose rushes in to pull her dad out of the way of the car.

The Doctor reacts in anger, recalling that when they first met Rose hadn't wanted to join him in his travels until he mentioned that the TARDIS was a time machine, implying that she'd long been plotting to do this. "I did it again," he says, "I picked another stupid ape. It's never about seeing the universe; it's about the universe doing something for you." This outburst is directed at Rose specifically but is also a larger observation about human selfishness.

The Tenth Doctor is eventually able to thwart the invading aliens in "The Christmas Invasion" after defeating their leader in a sword duel. Upon returning to the ship where the army has been waiting to invade, he tells them to leave. He also instructs them to not only talk about Earth's resources and potential when they visit other places, but also to mention that the planet is defended.

After this, the ship leaves peacefully of its own accord, honoring the terms of The Doctor's victory against their leader. The prime minister of Britain, who had been a witness to the entire ordeal, nevertheless orders a powerful laser to fire upon the departing ship, destroying it.

The Doctor is again angry, calling this an act of murder and pointing out that they were leaving. The prime minister tries to defend her actions, but The Doctor doesn't accept her explanation. He says he should have given the aliens a different warning: "I should have told them to run." The real monsters, he says, are the human race.

As The Twelfth Doctor becomes accustomed to his newly regenerated form in "Deep Breath," he at one point finds himself on a ledge overlooking Victorian London. As Clara and other companions approach to make sure he's okay, he reflects on what he sees. He comments that humanity could have been such a better species. Instead, in his words, they're "a planet of pudding brains." It's a comment made more out of pity and disappointment than anger or spite, as he seems to wonder why he continues to have so much regard for them.

This anger and disappointment never lasts. In each of these episodes, The Doctor ultimately continues to save and support humanity as best they can. Later in "Deep Breath," The Doctor confronts the villain as both of them climb into the sky on a spaceship. As they look down, The Doctor comments on the view from such a high angle, remarking that it's not beautiful, just far away. Up close, he says, all details are important. "Those people down there aren't small to me." Even for a planet full of "pudding brains," The Doctor expresses a desire to continue supporting and protecting it.

The Doctor sometimes seems to regret or wonder why they regard humanity so highly; why they're continually drawn to Earth to observe its history and help steer its future. At times humans act like monsters. They act out of their own self-interest instead of for the common good. At times they act like pudding brains instead of using their best capabilities to reason and build toward a better life for all.

But The Doctor also sees what can happen when humans act in their better nature, which The Doctor knows they're able to do. A species that has produced such great suffering and atrocity has also produced magnificent gains in art, science, and technology. And as often as people of Earth get it wrong, The Doctor keeps coming back because they know we can do amazing things when we get it right.

CHANGED BY A GIFT

Paul never calls anyone "pudding brains" in his letters, but he comes close at times. In the middle of his letter to the Galatians, he calls them foolish for wandering away from what he's been teaching them (Galatians 3:1) and later openly wonders if he's been wasting his time with them (4:11). He also expresses his wish that the people who have led them astray would castrate themselves (5:12).

Paul also has some strong words for the Corinthians when he calls out their spiteful and judgmental behavior toward one another. He points out practices in which some are engaging that are damaging to one another, mentioning them to shame the people practicing them (1 Corinthians 6:5). Shortly after, he shames them again by mentioning that as much as some in this community speak against defrauding others, they themselves are doing the same exact thing, "and believers, no less" (6:8, my paraphrase).

So Paul is not always happy with the behavior of his letter recipients. But that is one of the reasons he writes to them. He may use strong language to correct them at times, but he does so out of the knowledge that they can do better, and the hope that they will choose to do so. It is similar to what I once heard a seminary professor, the Rev. Dr. Marty Baumer, say to us during a class: "The reason the prophet Amos was so angry was because he loved his people so much." Paul is angry because he believes in and loves his people, and wishes better for them as they live and grow in faith and discipleship.

The theological foundation for Paul's approach is most clearly expressed in his letter to the Romans, which is considered his magnum opus, the letter that fleshes out the message that he has been writing and sharing with these various churches. The heart of the letter is his explanation of the relationship between sin, faith, and God's grace, and how these concepts interact in the life of the individual and in the life of a faith community.

In chapter 5 of this letter, Paul explains humanity's plight and God's initiative in reaching out to address it:

> For while we were still weak, at the right time Christ died for the ungodly. Indeed, rarely will anyone die for a righteous person—though perhaps for a good person someone might actually dare to die. But God proves his love for us in that while we still were sinners Christ died for us. Much more surely then, now that we have been justified by his blood, will we be saved through him from the wrath of God. For if while we were enemies, we were reconciled to God through the death of his Son, much more surely, having been reconciled, will we be saved by his life. But more than that, we even boast in God through our Lord Jesus Christ, through whom we have now received reconciliation. (Romans 5:6–11)

Paul connects Christ's death on the cross to God's love and salvation of ungodly—that is, people who are not following the ways of God in the world. Thus, there are twin concepts happening in this short passage.

The first is the presupposition that something has gone wrong between God and humanity. The relationship has become fractured, and the source of that fracturing has come from humanity's propensity to follow their own ways rather than what God would have us do and be in the world. Paul uses a varied vocabulary to describe the results: humanity is "ungodly," "sinners," and God's "enemies." Humanity is estranged from God due to a long history of bad decisions, ignorance, and disobedience.

The second is that the source and initiative of mending this relationship comes from God, specifically Jesus' death on the cross. "While we still were sinners Christ died for us" (5:8). This comes after Paul has pointed out how unusual it is for somebody to die even for a righteous or deserving person, let alone an ungodly or undeserving one. The idea in general is strange and rare, and yet

Christ in faithfulness went all the way to die on the cross for unfaithful humanity, which, in Paul's words, proves God's love. For God to do such an extraordinary thing through Jesus is a sign of God's commitment to healing the rift between Godself and human beings.

Even in the best of times, someone may not choose to put their life on the line for someone else. Whether due to instinct or self-preservation or rationalizing the cost, someone may not often make such an incredible sacrifice. This is part of what makes Paul's argument so powerful: God is willing to go above and beyond what most humans are willing to do. And by extension, it demonstrates a love far beyond human love as well.[1]

As Paul continues his explanation of what this means, however, he moves to the implications for how humanity is meant to live as a result:

> But the free gift is not like the trespass. For if the many died through the one man's trespass, much more surely have the grace of God and the free gift in the grace of the one man, Jesus Christ, abounded for the many. And the free gift is not like the effect of the one man's sin. For the judgment following one trespass brought condemnation, but the free gift following many trespasses brings justification. If, because of the one man's trespass, death exercised dominion through that one, much more surely will those who receive the abundance of grace and the free gift of righteousness exercise dominion in life through the one man, Jesus Christ. Therefore just as one man's trespass led to condemnation for all, so one man's act of righteousness leads to justification and life for all. For just as by the one man's disobedience the many were made sinners, so by the one man's obedience the many will be made righteous. But law came in, with the result that the trespass multiplied; but where sin increased, grace abounded all the more, so that, just as sin exercised dominion in death, so grace might also exercise dominion through justification leading to eternal life through Jesus Christ our Lord. (Romans 5:15–21)

---

1. Wright, "Letter to the Romans," 519.

Paul has just begun detailing his argument about how sin came into the world. The "one man" referenced in this passage is Adam, the first human being created in Genesis 2. He is the symbolic original ancestor of all humanity, along with his eventual partner, Eve. As Paul's reasoning goes, if all of humanity originates with Adam, then all of humanity's sinful nature originates with him as well. The power of sin over humanity began with Adam and Eve, and has been a burden to us ever since.[2]

The cause of that sinfulness that Adam began was his disobedience. Paul mentions the first man's trespass and disobedience throughout these verses, referring to the incident in Genesis where he and Eve ate the fruit of the one tree from which they were forbidden. By disobeying this command, the first humans introduced knowledge of good and evil, which brought with it condemnation and suffering for every generation that would follow.

The answer to this first human action of disobedience would be a second human act of obedience that would undo and overcome it. Paul names Christ as the "second Adam," one through whom God would work to correct what the first Adam did. This act of obedience was Jesus' willingness to be faithful all the way to death on the cross. Rather than turning away or opting out, Jesus followed the natural course of his life and ministry to be crucified by the world's powers. Not only would this act of complete obedience reverse Adam's earlier action, but it would overpower it through the introduction of God's grace freely given to humanity, which leads to new life.

This part of Paul's argument also includes a reference to the law. As with other letters, one of Paul's primary concerns with these different churches was to get them to see how God can work in the lives of people who don't adhere to the law. Here he points out that Adam and Eve predated the law, but once the law was established it did not fix the problem of sin. It could give people a different set of commands and guidelines to follow to help them avoid it, but it would not by itself correct it. Instead, it would take

---

2. Achtemeier, *Romans*, 96.

God's gracious gifts shared with humanity to set a new path for humanity to follow.[3]

The free gift is not like the trespass, Paul says. Rather, it is greater than the trespass.

After explaining how God has chosen to deal with sin through grace, Paul moves in the next chapter to its implications for how to live:

> What then are we to say? Should we continue in sin in order that grace may abound? By no means! How can we who died to sin go on living in it? Do you not know that all of us who have been baptized into Christ Jesus were baptized into his death? Therefore we have been buried with him by baptism into death, so that, just as Christ was raised from the dead by the glory of the Father, so we too might walk in newness of life. For if we have been united with him in a death like his, we will certainly be united with him in a resurrection like his. We know that our old self was crucified with him so that the body of sin might be destroyed, and we might no longer be enslaved to sin. For whoever has died is freed from sin. But if we have died with Christ, we believe that we will also live with him. We know that Christ, being raised from the dead, will never die again; death no longer has dominion over him. The death he died, he died to sin, once for all; but the life he lives, he lives to God. So you also must consider yourselves dead to sin and alive to God in Christ Jesus. (Romans 6:1–11)

At the beginning of this chapter, Paul asks what appears to be a rhetorical question, although it was probably a real issue that he had to address in these different churches. One natural conclusion that some may reach based on his argument about grace overcoming sin would be that since we're covered by the former, we can do as much of the latter as we want. This view treats grace as a perpetual "get out of jail free" card, which exhibits a lack of transformation on the individual's part who receives it. We see this issue arise in Paul's letter to the Corinthians, where he contends

3. Achtemeier, *Romans*, 98.

with people claiming that God's grace means that all things are permissible for them (1 Corinthians 6:12; 10:23).

To make his point, Paul uses the language of baptism, with which his readers and hearers would have been intimately familiar. The act of baptism in those earliest years would have taken place most often in a body of water, where new converts would have been lowered backward until submerged, much like some Christian traditions still observe today. This lowering would have symbolized death to one's old ways of living, including their sinful behavior. Likewise, their being raised back out of the water would have symbolized the new life that they were beginning. The act of baptism was a recreation of the story of Christ's death and resurrection playing out in the life of the one going through the ritual.

The implication, therefore, was that our old sinful ways no longer have control over us. Instead, the power of God's free gift realized through the cross and resurrection becomes humanity's new standard and inspiration for living. Grace has a transformative element to it, one that is ever moving us out of what damages the relationship between God, our neighbors, and ourselves, to one that heals and helps these relationships flourish instead.

God knows that humanity has lots of issues. Paul loses his patience with them at times, just as anyone else might. But these issues don't need to continue defining humanity's relationship to God, nor should they always have power over humanity's choices. God initiates a different way for humanity to follow, however imperfectly still, but one vastly different and more life-giving than what it had before.

CHANGING OUR VIEW

In his popular work *The Screwtape Letters*, C. S. Lewis imagines a series of letters written by a demon named Screwtape to his nephew Wormwood, who is on assignment to tempt and corrupt a particular human. In one of the earliest letters, Screwtape expresses his dismay that Wormwood's subject has converted to

Christianity and promises the usual punishments for such an egregious development.

Shortly after, Screwtape advises his charge on several ways that this may turn out to be useful to their efforts. And one of their chief allies in winning the man back, Screwtape says, will be the church itself. Their human subject may go through the usual passion and joy that comes when someone initially embraces the faith . . . but then they'll actually begin participating in a faith community, and this is where it may begin to fall apart. Why? Because he'll actually start interacting with other people.

Screwtape writes:

> When he goes inside, he sees the local grocer with rather an oily expression on his face bustling up to offer him one shiny little book containing a liturgy which neither of them understands, and one shabby little book containing corrupt texts of a number of religious lyrics, mostly bad, and in very small print. When he gets to his pew and looks round him he sees just that selection of his neighbors whom he has hitherto avoided. You want to lean pretty heavily on those neighbors. Make his mind flit to and fro between an expression like "the body of Christ" and the actual faces in the next pew. It matters very little, of course, what kind of people that next pew really contains. You may know one of them to be a great warrior on the Enemy's side. No matter. Your patient, thanks to Our Father Below, is a fool. Provided that any of those neighbours sing out of tune, or have boots that squeak, or double chins, or odd clothes, the patient will quite easily believe that their religion must therefore be somehow ridiculous.[4]

Screwtape's working theory is that once their subject bumps up against the imperfections and sins of other actual human beings, he'll lose his fervor and drift away from the entire Christian enterprise. He'll be tempted to give up and turn to other belief systems, or no particular system at all, to guide his life instead.

4. Lewis, *Screwtape Letters*, 22–23.

The Doctor faces this temptation on occasion. As often as they profess a belief in humanity's goodness and potential, there come instances when they are disappointed by specific choices that people make. For every time The Doctor is inspired by meeting great historical figures such as Vincent van Gogh, Nicola Tesla, or Rosa Parks, or expresses appreciation for something that their companions do to get them all out of trouble, there also come moments such as when Rose disrupts time or the prime minister orders an unnecessary act of violence.

When these later moments come, The Doctor sometimes wrestles with doubt about why they keep helping, why they keep inviting people onboard to see incredible things, why they keep returning to Earth. Why would they continue spending time with the pudding brains?

Paul becomes exasperated with his churches as well. He knows that they know better; he often wants them to act like it. But sometimes he can't help himself and unloads his frustration in his writing, calling them stupid and wondering why he keeps making the effort.

But both The Doctor and Paul know that there's more to the story than humanity's inevitable propensity to mess things up. For The Doctor, it's that potential that they keep mentioning: for every letdown, there's always the possibility that humanity can do amazing things for themselves and for others. And The Doctor has the added benefit of knowing what happens in the future; the ways that individuals and groups keep striving for new accomplishments and advances; how they keep trying to reach beyond themselves toward something greater, even if they won't be able to reap the benefits themselves. In the episode "The Lie of the Land," companion Bill Potts asks The Twelfth Doctor why he keeps putting up with humanity. The Doctor answers, "In the midst of seven billion, there's someone like you."

Paul believes something similar. Even if he sometimes voices how exasperated he is by something happening among his people, he much more often mentions how glad he is to hear about their faithful work, their perseverance, their deepening of understanding, their bearing of each other's struggles. He encourages them to continue striving for these greater acts of community and discipleship as best they can, even knowing that their best sometimes will fail.

After all, for Paul there's still God's grace. People may not always behave graciously. They may not always act as if they've truly died to an old destructive way of life while embracing the gift of resurrection. That gift is nevertheless ever present, from one flawed moment to the next, because even God intends us for better, life-giving things.

The Doctor and Paul sometimes have trouble seeing it. And as Lewis observes through Screwtape, we may have the same problem. For all that we hope and imagine for ourselves and for our neighbors, we're really good at getting it wrong. We seldom live up to the wonderful ideal image that we carry about humanity in our minds. But God keeps showing up, and in the times when we remember and live into that truth, we may be transformed a little bit more.

6

The Open Question of Redemption

As MANY DIFFERENT ALIEN species that The Doctor had battled on the show, it was inevitable that another Time Lord with evil intentions for the universe would arise for them to match wits with. Not all of The Doctor's fellow Gallifreans are noble or good, but the most cunning and ruthless one we are introduced to on the show goes by the title The Master.

The Master first appeared during The Third Doctor's tenure in a series of episodes titled "Terror of the Autons." We hear the familiar sound of the TARDIS outside of a carnival, although what appears is not the blue police box but a truck instead. Out steps a sinister-looking man dressed in black.

This first incarnation of The Master was played by Roger Delgado. His appearance is that of a typical villain, with black suits and a goatee. His manner is very formal, proper, and humorless. As "Terror of the Autons" progresses, we begin to learn more about his abilities. First, of course, we see that he has his own TARDIS with cloaking circuits that still work. He is also capable of hypnotizing people to do his bidding, just by maintaining eye contact with them and repeating commands.

Delgado's Master turns up often to do battle with The Third Doctor. When he does, the two hint at a familiarity with each other that goes back much further. In this initial series, for instance, The

Doctor warns of The Master's hypnotic powers before seeing them at work, and remarks to several characters at various points that his enemy's biggest weakness is vanity. Likewise, The Master comments on his admiration for The Doctor, even as he still considers him an adversary.

In "The Sea Devils," The Master has been imprisoned in a compound on an island. As The Third Doctor prepares to visit him, his companion Jo observes that The Doctor wanted to make sure he was okay. The Doctor responds that the two of them used to be good friends when they were growing up. After another of his plots is foiled in "The Daemons," The Doctor remarks to a captured Master that he'll deal with him later, and The Master replies, "You always were an optimist, weren't you?"

These earliest series establish that the dynamic between The Doctor and The Master is more complex than it is between The Doctor and other enemies. The two have a history that often causes The Doctor to look upon The Master with some degree of compassion and mercy, and the hope that his former friend can be reformed.

Not every interaction necessarily brings this to the forefront, however. In "The Deadly Assassin," for instance, The Fourth Doctor meets a version of The Master who has come to the end of his regeneration cycle and appears in an emaciated, skeletal form. The Master is plotting to frame The Doctor and destroy all his fellow Time Lords, and The Doctor's focus is not on reform but simply keeping him from carrying out his scheme. "You'd delay an execution to tear the wings off a fly," The Doctor comments at one point.

In the 1996 TV movie, The Master is played by Eric Roberts, an innocent bystander whose body is taken over by what is left of The Master's essence. Once again, The Master's appearance is what you'd expect a typical evildoer to look like: slicked-back hair, dark sunglasses, and a long leather trench coat. His powers of hypnosis once again play a prominent role in his scheme to steal The Eighth Doctor's remaining regenerations. As The Master is about to be sucked into a vortex, The Doctor offers his hand to save his adversary, but The Master refuses, his pride preventing him from receiving help.

The Master resurfaces in a trio of episodes during David Tennant's turn as The Tenth Doctor. In "Utopia," he and his companions meet an old scientist named Professor Yana, played by Derek Jacobi, who is helping a remnant of humanity build a rocket to escape a badly depleted Earth. The conversations between The Doctor and others begin triggering deeply suppressed memories for the professor, and it is finally revealed that Yana is The Master. At the end of the episode, he regenerates into a new form played by Jon Simm.

Simm's take on The Master is more of a zany, though no less ruthless, version of the character. He often makes jokes while he torments and schemes against others, showing a willingness to toy with his enemies that previous versions did not exhibit.

After we are reintroduced to The Master in "Utopia," in the two subsequent episodes, "The Sound of Drums" and "Last of the Time Lords," his past with The Doctor comes back to the forefront as a key component of their interactions. The Master reflects on the Time Lords making him look into the Untempered Schism—the source of the Time Lords' power—when he was a child, which was what made him go mad. Before the Time War began, the Time Lords resurrected him because they saw him as a key warrior in defeating the Daleks. This again plays to The Doctor's sympathy, as he again expresses a desire to help. As he tells another character, "I'm not here to kill him, I'm here to save him."

Peter Capaldi's time as The Twelfth Doctor features one of the most intriguing turns in The Master's history. During the first season with this incarnation, we meet a mysterious woman named Missy, played by Michelle Gomez. She is eventually revealed to be the regenerated Master, with "Missy" being short for "Mistress." Gomez also plays the character as preferring to have fun with her victims while simultaneously tormenting them.

Missy and The Doctor's history is again brought to the forefront in a series of episodes beginning with "Extremis," which shows a captured Missy being led to her execution. The Doctor has been obliged to carry out her fate, and he openly expresses hesitation and reserve about doing so. Likewise, Missy pleads with

The Doctor to show mercy and to help her become good, even appealing to their friendship. The Doctor agrees.

The episodes "World Enough and Time" and "The Doctor Falls" feature Missy hitting a roadblock in her reform efforts. The Doctor has continued to work with her, but John Simm's Master has also returned, and she is caught in the middle between her old ways and her desires to change. We are initially led to believe that Missy has given up on her new path, only to see later that she was plotting against her past form the entire time. Simm's Master expresses disgust at this turn of events, and Missy responds that this is where it's all been going, and that it's time for her to stand with The Doctor at long last. The Master blasts her with his laser screwdriver, preferring to stop all future regenerations than for any future form to do so.

As mentioned and illustrated, The Master has the most complicated relationships with The Doctor out of any threat on the show. The Twelfth Doctor refers to Missy as his oldest friend in the universe, and we see that affect their dynamic in different ways throughout the show's history. When others want to exact severe punishment on The Master for what he did in "The Sound of Drums" and "Last of the Time Lords," The Doctor rebuffs their threats and wants to imprison him in the hope of changing him instead. After one of them makes good on their desires, The Master refuses to regenerate, choosing death over repentance yet again.

The presence of a character like The Master in *Doctor Who* invites questions of whether anyone is truly beyond redemption. They often commit unspeakable acts and leave so much destruction and chaos behind them. But while others quickly move to wanting vengeance in response, The Doctor believes that they are capable of changing, even as The Master refuses time and time again.

Just as The Master once poses the question to The Doctor, so we may also ask: is it worth being so optimistic? Are some people simply beyond the possibility of reforming?

THE STRUGGLE TO FORGIVE

One of the most scandalous moments shared between The Doctor and The Master occurs near the end of "Last of the Time Lords." The Master's plot has been foiled by The Doctor and his companions, and The Master is recoiling in fear and frustration as he realizes his failure and being outnumbered by those working against him. He shrinks against a wall, cowering with his hands over his head.

The Doctor approaches him, and The Master seems to know what's coming and doesn't want it to happen. But The Doctor persists, getting closer and closer to his former friend until they are side by side. The Doctor then leans down, embraces him, and says, "I forgive you."

I name this scene as "scandalous" for a few reasons. First, in the context of the episode, The Doctor's actions are repulsive to many of the other characters, several of whom have vowed death upon The Master for the suffering that he has caused them personally, as well as the havoc he has inflicted upon the world. They are not in a mental or emotional state to forgive and would rather see their enemy punished for what he has done. They don't seem to believe that he is worth forgiving; that his actions are beyond such gestures, at least in the immediate moment.

Second is the scandal that this may cause for the viewer. Some may watch this scene and feel inspired, taking it as a parable for what we may strive to do toward people in our own lives who have wronged or hurt us in some way. Others, however, may see this scene through the same lens as many of the other characters, counting the cost of what The Master has done against the three words that The Doctor utters, seeing this as a trivialization of what happened prior to it.

If we truly stop to consider the significance of The Master's treachery in this series of episodes, there may be little blame that we may be able to place both on the characters and viewers who react this way. It may be easy to understand if we are able to name our own struggles with forgiveness, and how much easier it is to talk about or encourage others to do than it is to show in practice.

On July 7, 2005, four bombs were set off in London that killed over fifty people. One of the people murdered in those attacks was a young woman named Jenny Nicholson. Jenny's mother, Julie, was an ordained vicar in the Anglican Church, serving a congregation in Bristol. Shortly after the death of her daughter, Nicholson resigned her pastorate, citing her inability to forgive the bombers for what they did.

"It's very difficult to stand behind an altar and lead people in words of peace and reconciliation and forgiveness when I feel very far from that myself," she said at the time.[1] The words of forgiveness may be easy to talk about, but to be able to show it to another requires a great deal of personal searching and healing, let alone facing the person again in order to share it.

There are a series of in-between steps that could make forgiveness and reconciliation possible. For the victim, this may include any number of activities that tend to their physical, emotional, and spiritual wounds such as therapy, medication, removing oneself from the environment where the damage was done, finding support from others, and so on. This process could take years, or even the rest of one's life, for that inner space to finally be cultivated.

There are also a series of steps that the perpetrator would need to make. The criticism of The Doctor rushing to hug The Master lies in how quickly it happens, before The Master shows any remorse or moves to make things right between himself and others. In similar fashion, those who have hurt or abused or exploited others have to go about their own process of changing what inside them led to their actions. Their victims and others still may never see them as trustworthy again, but the desire and subsequent efforts to change is an important piece of the process regardless.

A term sometimes used to describe this process of change is "redemption." It is a transactional term with roots in banking and commerce, where one may receive clearance from a debt. When applied to personal relationships, it is usually used to imply that the one who has done wrong is now in debt to the other, and in

---

1. Vallely, "Vicar Struggles to Forgive."

order to redeem oneself or the relationship, one must take a series of steps to change oneself and mend the damage.

Part of what changes in the redemption process is how one sees the other. In the short term, one who has been wronged by another will see the perpetrator primarily in terms of what they have done. One of the things that may change over time is that perception, where they may again become more to their victim than what they had done. But the weight and length of such a change cannot be minimized, by both parties involved and by others hoping for redemption as well.

For Rev. Nicholson, no redemption was possible. For The Doctor, it was possible for The Master, and he perhaps saw that initial speaking of "I forgive you" to be a moment that might inspire him to begin to change. For everyone else, a moment may eventually come, though it is not guaranteed and in many cases if it does come, it may bring caveats to ensure safety. Could The Master and others be seen or trusted as more than their hurtful actions? That is a question to be answered individually by those on both sides, and the two may or may not ever meet in a middle space.

PAUL AND THE FREE GIFT

The letters attributed to Paul in the New Testament only mention the concept of forgiveness a handful of times. A form of the verb "to forgive" turns up once in Romans, and that's only because he's quoting Psalm 32:1. One instance of "forgiveness" turn up in Ephesians and Colossians. And that's the end of the list.[2]

For Paul, forgiveness is not the primary issue when it comes to being in good standing with God, with one's community, or with another individual. He seems much more interested in the concept of justification, a word that turns up much more often in his writings, such as in Romans 3:

> Now we know that whatever the law says, it speaks to
> those who are under the law, so that every mouth may

2. Stendahl, *Paul Among Jews and Gentiles*, 23–24.

be silenced, and the whole world may be held account-
able to God. For "no human being will be justified in his
sight" by deeds prescribed by the law, for through the
law comes the knowledge of sin. But now, apart from
law, the righteousness of God has been disclosed, and is
attested by the law and the prophets, the righteousness
of God through faith in Jesus Christ for all who believe.
For there is no distinction, since all have sinned and fall
short of the glory of God; they are now justified by his
grace as a gift, through the redemption that is in Christ
Jesus, whom God put forward as a sacrifice of atonement
by his blood, effective through faith. He did this to show
his righteousness, because in his divine forbearance he
had passed over the sins previously committed; it was to
prove at the present time that he himself is righteous and
that he justifies the one who has faith in Jesus. Then what
becomes of boasting? It is excluded. By what law? By that
of works? No, but by the law of faith. For we hold that a
person is justified by faith apart from works prescribed
by the law. Or is God the God of Jews only? Is he not the
God of Gentiles also? Yes, of Gentiles also, since God is
one; and he will justify the circumcised on the ground of
faith and the uncircumcised through that same faith. Do
we then overthrow the law by this faith? By no means!
On the contrary, we uphold the law. (Romans 3:19–31)

There are hints in this passage of a recurring argument that
Paul often has in his letters about inclusion of Gentiles in the new
Jesus-following community, which are more sharply drawn in other
places. The references here to the law are part of that argument,
where some insist that keeping of the Mosaic law is essential to acceptance into the community, while Paul and others push back and
say that God is using a different metric, namely grace through faith.

In the first part of this passage, Paul identifies a problem
common to all humanity: all are sinners. All are prone to thoughts,
words, and deeds of selfishness, self-idolatry, ignoring of others'
needs, intentional harm done to others, and so on. "There is no
distinction . . . all have sinned and fall short of the glory of God"
(3:22b–23). In the eyes of God, there are no favorites on this:

everyone has to answer for how they have not lived up to the ideals set by God by which to live in the world.

For Paul, all have the same standing before God. A set of rules or buildup of capital through good works will not put some on a higher platform than others, which some in Paul's day were trying to do through their own theological reasoning. In that sense, the groups that Paul is attempting to reconcile into one community are already unified.[3]

The language that Paul uses to describe this standing is justification. As mentioned, Paul barely mentions the concept of forgiveness; in contrast, the concept of justification is mentioned about fifty times.[4] It is a much more significant issue for him, in part because he wanted to reconcile people into a single community without preferences or tiers of belonging.

To be justified in the eyes of God or others was to have a status of full belonging. We may each be familiar with organizations or less formal groups that carry with them the expectation that one adhere to a certain guideline in order to have good standing with the rest of the people involved. So long as you live up to a specified standard, your participation and privilege to belong is justified in the eyes of everyone else.

Paul's argument against those who wish to maintain a guideline to justify one's belonging is that no one is justified in the eyes of God. Everyone has issues with sin; everyone has given themselves preference at another's expense or exploited or abused one's fellow humans in one form or another. And just as no one may justify themselves, so too are all in need of the same justification from someplace else.

Now comes the second part of Paul's argument. Just as it turns out all are united in the same lack of self-justification and inability to move up the ladder by one's own merits, so too are all united by the same source that is able to change that situation: God's grace.

The term "grace" implies something that is given and received, rather than earned or achieved. After naming the problem

---

3. Borg and Crossan, *First Paul*, 162.

4. Stendahl, *Paul Among Jews and Gentiles*, 27.

in verse 23, Paul moves to the solution in verse 24: "they are now justified by his grace *as a gift*, through the redemption that is in Christ Jesus." God is freely giving a gift of justification to all who receive it and live by it in faith. And this is what justifies; what changes one's standing, rather than anything one strives to do to make one worthy on one's own.

In order to drive the point home that he's serious about this concept of justification via a free gift offered by God, Paul repeats it through most of Romans 5, repeating the phrase "free gift" five times in the span of three verses, 15–17. He wants his readers and hearers to understand that what God offers to all of humanity equally is freely given.

At this point, it is worth mentioning three things about the free gift that Paul mentions so thoroughly in Romans. First is the nature of how that gift came about, that being through the life, death, and resurrection of Jesus. The cross of Christ is a key event for Paul for several reasons, among them it being the sign of God's self-giving love, shown in Jesus' obedience and love for both God and humanity by seeing it through all the way to his death. For Paul, Christ is the sign, the person, the action through which God shows and shares this free gift, justifies all, and gives everyone the same standing in the new community.

The second is that the nature of a gift is that it is offered and received. One does not earn a gift. It is given at the discretion and according to the love of the giver. At the same time, a gift is not given until it is received by the one to whom it is given. We may not want the gift being offered, and may instead leave it, return it, or ignore it. This does not alter what the giver does, only what the intended recipient does with it.

Finally, a gift is transformative. It doesn't leave us as we are, but instead inspires us to a response of gratitude. In the case of God's justification by grace, this entails a lifetime of intentional living and self-giving that all stems from that initial gift given. We change and live differently not to continually make ourselves worthy of the gift, but out of gratitude for the grace first shown to us.

Paul's case for justification includes reminding his audience that all begin with the same need for forgiveness and redemption. As a solution, all are offered the same gift through Christ: new life, new belonging, and renewed standing and identity. And when this free gift is received, it will inspire further change over time for those who accept it.

THE HOPE OF JUSTIFICATION AND REDEMPTION

When Paul writes in Romans about God's free gift of grace that leads to justification, he ties it to redemption specifically revealed in the cross of Christ. As mentioned earlier in the chapter, redemption is tied to the paying of a debt; the freeing of someone from what they owe to another.

In other words, redemption is about freedom. To be redeemed is to be freed from something in which we are currently trapped. As Marcus Borg and John Dominic Crossan have observed, when Paul wrote about "the redemption that is in Christ Jesus," it could have been better translated "the liberation that is in Christ Jesus."[5]

The cross means a lot to Paul, and among other things it means liberation. When he wrote about God redeeming us, he was talking about God freeing us from former things in which we were trapped in order to be freed into the transformed life inspired and defined by the grace that God offers as a free gift. These former things include old attitudes and actions that are destructive and demeaning to God, to others, and to ourselves. Receiving this gift of liberation begins one's journey of moving from the old to the new.

At the conclusion of "Last of the Time Lords," The Doctor offers forgiveness and a chance for The Master to begin his own process of redemption while they ride together on the TARDIS. The Master chooses not to receive this gift, instead refusing to regenerate and live on according to the free gift offered to him.

---

5. Borg and Crossan, *First Paul*, 146.

It serves as his final act of spite toward The Doctor and to other survivors of the harm that he has inflicted upon the world.

After The Master returns as Missy and is spared from execution by The Doctor, she seems to take this journey much more seriously, and to be open to the gift previously offered. In "The Doctor Falls," she admits to her former incarnation that she has finally accepted the gift, and has been attempting to put old ways behind her to embrace a new transformed life. She has accepted redemption for herself, and has only begun to journey toward justification in the eyes of others.

Unfortunately for Missy, this journey is short-lived. But after so many attempts by The Doctor throughout the series to bring The Master to this point, we see that it was possible all along.

Could such a possibility exist for other individuals or groups who have perpetrated harm on another? There might always be hope for such redemption and justification, although it would not come without great soul-searching and confession, as well as making amends toward others as necessary.

The theologian Miroslav Volf observes that aggressor and victim alike are in need of liberation from what has occurred between them. Perpetrators need liberation from what led them to commit harm toward another, be it an exclusionary or discriminatory worldview, selfishness, or abusive attitudes. Victims may need liberation from thoughts of revenge, but moreso from the trauma that has been inflicted on their body, mind, and spirit.[6]

Any act of forgiveness or redemption must include justice. It begins with a free gift offered by God that soothes and heals the ways one is oppressed and reforms the ways one oppresses others. Inasmuch as one receives it gratefully, there may always be hope for this gift to lead to reconciliation and peace between those who need it in different ways.

6. Volf, *Exclusion and Embrace*, 120.

7

Unified, Not Assimilated

THE CYBERMEN ARE ANOTHER of The Doctor's most recurring foes, and have been so since the beginning. They first appeared in the series "The Tenth Planet," opposite William Hartnell's first incarnation of The Doctor. In this series, The Doctor and his companions Polly and Ben land outside a military base at the South Pole and are quickly taken into custody. At the same time, the group stationed there is exploring and analyzing the discovery of a new planet in the solar system that looks remarkably similar to Earth. The Doctor seems to know something about this planet already, yet plays coy about his knowledge, only revealing that he knows the base will soon be visited by this planet's inhabitants.

Sure enough, the Cybermen appear, having quickly infiltrated the base and overtaken the soldiers in the main control room. The Cyberman designated to speak for the others explains who they are, including naming the Earth-identical planet as Mondas, which was once inhabited by humans just like on Earth. Over time, the Cyberman explains, their doctors and scientists began seeking ways to prolong their species' lifespan, devising the solution of replacing body parts with electronic and metal parts instead, until all that remained was the brain.

The Cyberman further explains that along with this replacement of limbs and organs came a removal of weaknesses. When pressed to say more about what it means by "weakness," it names emotion. "We do not fear pain," it says, implying that emotion only brings pain, and to remove the ability to feel is to remove the possibility of that becoming a hindrance in any way.

This theme of emotion as weakness endures whenever the Cybermen return to further torment The Doctor in subsequent series and episodes. When Patrick Troughton's second incarnation of The Doctor encounters them in "The Invasion" and "Tomb of the Cybermen," their boasting of not having fear, pain, and feelings to hold them back is as prominent as it was in "The Tenth Planet."

In these later encounters, however, the Cybermen pursue a stated goal that is mentioned more in passing in the earlier one, but is much more of their primary intention in these later ones: to convert humans into more Cybermen.

In "Tomb of the Cybermen," The Second Doctor and his companions Jamie and Victoria encounter an archeological expedition seeking the final resting place of the Cybermen. This group is partially led and funded by Eric Klieg, who wants to take control of the Cybermen for his own means. Once the Cybermen are thawed from their frozen tomb, however, they have other ideas, including transforming every human who has come to release them. Their haunting robotic refrain of "you will be like us" recurs throughout this confrontation.

A similar story plays out in "The Invasion," where this time the one intending to take control of the Cybermen's presence is Tobias Vaughn, the head of a tech company that already regulates most of Earth's technology usage (imagine Amazon or Apple being even more powerful and omnipresent than they already are). Once again, it is The Second Doctor who steps in to unveil Vaughn's conspiracy to bring the Cybermen to Earth.

Much like Klieg in "Tomb of the Cybermen," Vaughn discovers that using the Cybermen for his own ends is much more difficult than he imagined. The Cybermen insist that, as part of their deal, he must be converted to a Cyberman himself, which he resists. And, unlike Klieg, Vaughn has a contingency plan in the form of a device to cause Cybermen to feel emotions, which we see debilitates them in later parts of this series.

While the Cybermen make many appearances over the span of *Doctor Who*, their multiple encounters with David Tennant's Tenth Doctor might rank among some of their most memorable. In the two-part story "Rise of the Cybermen" and "The Age of Steel," The Doctor and his companions Rose and Mickey land in a parallel version of Earth and discover a plot similar to "The Invasion." This time, the corrupt tech mogul is John Lumic, who has intentions of converting people to Cybermen himself rather than work with an outside force. As in previous descriptions of the process, human brains are extracted and placed in a metal exoskeleton, which Lumic deems "the ultimate upgrade." The use of "upgrade" reiterates the Cybermen belief that humans in their present form are inferior due to how our bodies wear out and our experience of emotion. Later, when the Cybermen begin enacting their plot to upgrade humans, they deem it compulsory, with those who refuse being "deleted."

When The Doctor first realizes whom he's up against, he tries to describe what the Cybermen are to Rose, and Rose asks why they have their emotions taken away. The Doctor simply answers, "because it hurts." This is proven in the second part of the story, as it is revealed that Cybermen have an emotional inhibitor that can be removed. The Doctor's way of defeating them involves removing that inhibitor, which causes them to realize what they've become. "I gave them back their souls," he says, with equal degrees of triumph and sadness.

These same Cybermen return in a later Tenth Doctor two-part story, "Army of Ghosts" and "Doomsday," where they find a way to travel from their alternate reality into this one. As they begin overtaking the populace, they again proclaim their intentions to convert them: "You need not fear. Cybermen will remove fear. Cybermen will remove sex and class and color and creed. You will become identical. You will become like us." This restates their view of conversion as upgrade; that all removal of difference in appearance, status, belief, and emotion is superior to humanity as it currently is.

Like many recurring monsters on *Doctor Who*, the goals of the Cybermen don't really vary from one appearance to another. They are always governed by a belief that their uniformity in thought and physical form is preferable to human difference, and that emotion is a weakness to be removed. And this belief compels them to convert or upgrade others to their existence, and to destroy those who resist. In their robotic eyes, to be equal is to be the same, to be strong is to not feel or fear, and to live is to obey.

BLENDING IN TO BELONG

Many may be able to identify why the Cybermen's point of view is problematic. Right off the bat, of course, the show sets up their goals as sinister and wrong, and their approach is so over the top as to be seen as something to fear, resist, and fight back against. The Cybermen do not want merely to force others to think more like them or dress more in line with what they prefer or act in certain ways that they approve of. Instead, they want all of humanity to look, talk, act, think, and feel (or not feel) exactly like they do, without variation or nuance. Rather than try to convert people to a different belief system or code of conduct, they aim to eliminate all possibility of alternatives and all capability of considering them.

The Cybermen view difference as a flaw, and their answer to such a flaw is to remove it in one of two ways: forcing humanity into bodies and programming that force them to conform, or elimination. You will be either "upgraded" or "deleted," and there are no other options.

Fans of other franchises may be able to identify this same idea presented in other ways. One may think of the Borg in *Star Trek*, or Agent Smith in *The Matrix* sequels. Each of these also insist on complete conformity, to the point of forcing people to think or to look exactly like they do. The Cybermen and these other examples serve as visual parables for the downside of coercing everyone to adhere to a singular system without even the possibility of digression.

These serve as visual parables because they show the natural consequence of such coercion and insistence. They invite the viewer to ask where the limit is when wishing for others to adhere to standards of belief or conduct in order to belong.

A group or community may define itself by certain parameters that can be useful and guard against voices or behavior that may threaten its identity or cohesion. Many do this to protect their members and to resist the possibility of abuse. For many such groups that have been formed to be safe havens for persecuted minorities or places of healing and recovery, such rules are needed.

The Cybermen are not such a group. Instead, they represent the sort of institutions and organizations that use power to force not just compliance, but consistency. Rather than exist as a space for respite, they move into worlds to overtake them and make them identical in every literal way. They raise questions for real groups with any semblance of power and privilege to ask themselves about their own tactics and how far their own rules and standards are meant to reach, both in theory and in practice. And, in fact, these power groups are the reason why many groups serving as places of safety or healing exist.

If a group has ten rules and a member is able to adhere to all but one, where does that person stand with the group? What happens to them until they are able to "correct" themselves regarding that single point? How do others in the group treat that person in the meantime? Are all ten rules weighted the same, considered equally critical to belonging? How might the group benefit or learn or evolve thanks to that difference, and what might it be missing out on when it insists on elimination instead? What sort of physical, emotional, psychological, and spiritual toll does the policing of difference take both on the enforcers and the people trying to live up to what the group wants?

Via the Cybermen, *Doctor Who* shows us the extreme version of choosing elimination over learning or evolving. In fact, the Cybermen consider themselves the finished product of evolution, the "ultimate upgrade," over which there is nothing higher. They are indifferent to any harm that they inflict upon others because their beliefs are absolute and they even consider compassion and compromise weaknesses.

History is littered with examples of the violent consequences of eliminating difference for the sake of all people thinking, believing, or looking the same. Such instances serve as large and public examples of how what *Doctor Who* presents with the Cybermen is not all that far-fetched or removed from the human experience, even though our track record of learning from past instances of large-scale forced conformity is spotty at best.

But we may also consider smaller examples of communities that insist on similarity of belief and behavior under implicit or explicit threat of ostracizing those who diverge from its rules and wishes.

I was once involved with a ministry that touted itself as non-denominational, although many observers probably would have identified it as evangelical or conservative in belief and practice. At the beginning of my time with them, my beliefs were very similar to the stated or unspoken standards of the group, and I was even counted among its leadership for a time.

There came a point, however, where my own beliefs began to diverge from that of the larger organization. There were several factors that contributed to this. The first was a series of faith questions that began to echo louder and louder in my own mind and spirit, and were not easily resolved by the answers provided by my fellow members. The second was my increased discomfort with how I saw others from this group treating those who disagreed with them, which frequently was hurtful and alienating.

When I began to push back against some of this behavior, I started to notice a change in the group's attitude toward me. Once part of the center, I felt myself increasingly pushed outward toward the edges. There was never a blatant Cyberman-like insistence on changing myself. Rather, the tactics were much more passive-aggressive. There were almost certainly conversations about me beyond my hearing or knowing, but the methods employed in my presence were subtle. And yet the basic message conveyed was the same: if you fall back in line, this will stop and we will welcome you again. Otherwise, feel free to move on.

I could write an entire separate book about the effect that this series of events had on me both as they happened and for a while after. The ways that groups enforce conformity do not have to be outwardly menacing in order to be violent or traumatic. It is not just a Cyberman-style approach that can be effective at making people blend in to belong.

What's the alternative? Can a group hold together without such an insistence on sameness? That was one of the main questions that Paul wrestled with.

WHEN UNITY THREATENS COMMUNITY

While Paul never had to face a threat like the Cybermen, he did have to argue against similar ideas present in some of the communities he wrote to. His letter to the Galatians shows that the issue of whether to conform to certain standards of identity in order to belong was particularly prevalent. And more than once, the issue at hand is so urgent and such a point of passion for Paul that he allows his emotions on the matter to spill onto the page.

The opening chapter of Galatians immediately has Paul on the defensive. There are other missionaries who have visited this faith community, and are, according to Paul, proclaiming a "different gospel" (1:6–7). As part of their message, they are also making attempts to discredit Paul's authority as an apostle, which causes Paul to remind his hearers and readers of his calling from God multiple times in this opening chapter (1:1–2, 11–24). He has to address the problem on various fronts at once.

The heart of the problem is spelled out at the beginning of chapter 5:

> Listen! I, Paul, am telling you that if you let yourselves be circumcised, Christ will be of no benefit to you. Once again I testify to every man who lets himself be circumcised that he is obliged to obey the entire law. You who want to be justified by the law have cut yourselves

off from Christ; you have fallen away from grace. For through the Spirit, by faith, we eagerly wait for the hope of righteousness. For in Christ Jesus neither circumcision nor uncircumcision counts for anything; the only thing that counts is faith working through love. You were running well; who prevented you from obeying the truth? Such persuasion does not come from the one who calls you. A little yeast leavens the whole batch of dough. I am confident about you in the Lord that you will not think otherwise. But whoever it is that is confusing you will pay the penalty. But my friends, why am I still being persecuted if I am still preaching circumcision? In that case the offense of the cross has been removed. I wish those who unsettle you would castrate themselves!

For you were called to freedom, brothers and sisters; only do not use your freedom as an opportunity for self-indulgence, but through love become slaves to one another. For the whole law is summed up in a single commandment, "You shall love your neighbor as yourself." If, however, you bite and devour one another, take care that you are not consumed by one another. (Galatians 5:2–15)

This other group of apostles has insisted that in order for non-Jews to be included in this new Way of Jesus faith, male members must become circumcised as part of their conversion. Circumcision is a requirement in the Mosaic law, and some among the Galatians are considering taking this step to become what these other missionaries have deemed true members of the faith. In this sense, the message of these missionaries is similar to the Cybermen: "You will become like us." Circumcision is an upgrade over their previous existence as followers and believers in Jesus. Their trust may have been commendable, but observing this next step would bring them into greater acceptance in the eyes of those proclaiming this as essential. In fact, some in the Galatian community have already begun observing festivals and special days as a result of this group's insistence on greater conformity (4:10–11), but this move toward circumcision is significant enough for Paul to devote this entire letter to countering this creeping belief.

In the quoted passage from chapter 5, Paul names the risk in taking this step. He argues that if the Galatians—who were justified in God's eyes already—wish to further justify themselves by taking on a requirement of the Torah, then they will have to observe the entire Torah (5:3). The law is not an exercise in picking and choosing what to keep and what to ignore; rather it is all or nothing.

Paul no doubt wrote this with appreciation and affection for the law rather than disdain, given his upbringing as a Jewish believer and his status as a Pharisee. His understanding of God's calling for himself is to proclaim Christ to Gentiles, and that proclamation includes the provision that Gentile converts would not have to convert first to Judaism before converting to Christianity. His interest in this letter is to argue that there is no middle step for those who have not already taken it: there are no upgrades that one has to make first.

When Paul argues in verse 6 that "in Christ Jesus neither circumcision nor uncircumcision counts for anything," he is saying that there is something greater beyond the specifics of human anatomy or practice that holds the community of Christ together. It is "faith working through love" that is paramount over any specific differences among people seeking to be faithful, and one does not have to further conform prior to receiving acceptance.

Lest anyone misunderstand what this entails, Paul offers some clarifications in verses 13–15. "You were called to freedom," he writes, meaning both freedom from a former way of living according to harmful desires and attitudes and from any expectations of seeking further uniformity. However, he warns, that freedom does not come with a blank check to do whatever one pleases (an issue another community he wrote to, the Corinthians, had a serious problem understanding). Instead, in Christ one is freed from these old ways of living and these ongoing expectations from certain groups, but also freed for a binding into a new kind of community, where trust in Christ is the main and only signifier of belonging, and love for one another is the primary expression of that trust.

This is the "faith working through love" that Paul mentions at the beginning of this passage. Rather than achieve some physical conformity as a prerequisite, the only requirement to belong is to strive alongside one another with a common belief that Christ has called us together to live in support with one another. Such support includes both encouragement and accountability around what that calling entails. But for Paul, the only needed upgrade for the Galatians and others to belong to this new Christ-following movement is trust in Christ expressed in love for others.

LEARNING FROM DIFFERENCE

The main difference between Paul and The Doctor's situations is that in *Doctor Who* hardly anybody aspires to be a Cyberman. The rare exception is John Lumic, the villain in "Rise of the Cybermen" and "Age of Steel," who sees being converted into one of their metal bodies as preferable to his own deteriorating physical health. His belief in their superiority fuels his plot to upgrade everyone else. However, he still voices his resistance to being converted when the Cybermen choose his moment for him: he yells "not yet!" as they force him into the chamber that will give him his new form. Once he faces the reality of being made a Cyberman himself, he has second thoughts despite his previously voiced views that their situation is preferable.

So even for someone like Lumic, the process of being made a Cyberman is something that is forced upon him. Every time The Doctor encounters them, his primary aim is to thwart their efforts to make others become like them. Not only is the nature of their goal involuntary, but it is also violent as they rob people of their unique bodies and personalities.

For communities like the Galatians in Paul's day, their members are much more receptive to the message that he and his fellow workers share. He proclaims among them inclusion in a new type of family based on God's grace shown through Christ. His proclamation is based on an invitation rather than forced conversion, which is what makes it good news.

For Paul, it only becomes bad news when other apostles begin tacking on extra requirements for belonging. When the Galatians begin hearing that receiving God's grace is not enough and that they must also observe parts of the Mosaic law, that is when he begins writing letters defending his own calling and pleading with a community he loves not to heed messages that require more of them for belonging than they need. They've already done enough to belong; now their mutual calling to build one another up and serve others begins.

In her book *Searching for Sunday*, Rachel Held Evans reflects on the sacrament of Communion, the act of remembering Jesus' final meal with his disciples before his death. It is also an act of remembering Jesus' continued presence and sharing of God's grace with those who partake. An open table reflects God's open welcome of all, without having to make oneself acceptable first. Unfortunately, she observes, there are many who prefer to engage in what she calls a "border patrol Christianity," where people judge whether one has become similar enough in order to belong:

> But the gospel doesn't need a coalition devoted to keeping the wrong people out. It needs a family of sinners, saved by grace, committed to tearing down the walls, throwing open the doors, and shouting, "Welcome! There's bread and wine. Come eat with us and talk." This isn't a kingdom for the worthy; it's a kingdom for the hungry.[1]

Both The Doctor and Paul are battling the mentality that one must make oneself more worthy before they may be able to find acceptance. This state of worthiness involves becoming more like those standing at the gates; those with the power to welcome others into fellowship.

The Cybermen see variations such as gender, race, and belief as problems to be removed, rather than opportunities to learn from one another and enrich one's understanding of the world. Both in Paul's day and in so many historical examples right up to the present, people in the church have often demanded a uniformity in order to belong, with many physical, emotional, and spiritual casualties in their wake.

---

1. Evans, *Searching for Sunday*, 149.

And yet it is the differences among members that make any such fellowship remarkable. The Doctor sees humanity's imperfections and capacity to feel as qualities to celebrate. Paul seemed not only to know but to appreciate what it meant for people of different backgrounds to all be covered under the same divine gifts of grace and forgiveness offered to all without prerequisite.

Of course, nobody who has ever attempted to be in relationship with others will say that it's easy. Preferences and habits and experiences and worldviews inevitably tug and push at a community, always presenting a choice of whether to continue or break things off. And at times, such a choice may hinge on a spoken or implied demand to conform more closely to someone else's practice or perspective.

Both The Doctor and Paul know the messiness of relationship, and in their own ways they celebrate that messiness as a gift. That messiness is inherent in human difference, and the challenge of relationship involves recognizing one another's value even in light of such difference.

For people of faith in particular, that value is rooted in all being created and beloved by God, even before conscious acceptance of a particular way of belief or life. But for those who seek Christian community in particular, Paul points out that God's grace, which inspires a life of faith expressed through love, is enough to belong. Anything in addition risks placing a burden on one another that God didn't intend.

8

Companions Make a Difference

In the vast majority of The Doctor's adventures through time and space, they very rarely travel alone. Much more often, they have one or more companions to accompany them. These companions have varied in number, gender, and species, but they often prove to be essential for The Doctor's journey.

The Doctor hardly ever has a strategy for inviting companions to travel with them. Usually it is a matter of circumstance that leads to their tagging along for a while. The typical beginning to a companion's travels on the TARDIS involves their becoming swept up into their first adventure as an innocent bystander; they get to know The Doctor over the course of their resolving the issue, and they're either invited or invite themselves into The Doctor's life for a time.

What each companion adds to The Doctor's journey depends upon the personalities, experience, talents, and interests of each. Any one companion, of course, will fulfill multiple roles in The Doctor's life at a time. But we can categorize what they add to The Doctor's story in a few general ways.

First, many companions serve as the eyes through which the viewer interprets The Doctor's actions. This has been their primary function going all the way back to the show's earliest days. As most companions are human, they watch The Doctor at work, ask questions, and stand amazed at what they are able to witness as a result of hitching a ride along with their new alien friend.

One example comes in "The Power of the Daleks," the first series where The First Doctor has regenerated into the Second. It is both their and the viewers' first experience of this concept, and The Doctor's companions Polly and Ben spend a great deal of time early on trying to understand what has happened. They observe not only changes to his appearance, but also to his mannerisms. At one point, Polly just outright exclaims, "It's not just his face that's changed; he doesn't even act like him!" In this line, she might be voicing what people watching the show are thinking, and helping them interpret it.

Another example is Josephine Grant, who is assigned by UNIT to work with The Third Doctor. Beginning from her appearance in "Terror of the Autons," she often watches on in wide-eyed wonder at what The Doctor says and does, and tries her best to keep up as she encounters new and strange things that are more familiar to him. She and The Doctor sometimes have a contentious relationship, as her questions and attempts to understand are sometimes dismissed as if the answers are the most obvious things in the universe. Jo is an audience surrogate, sometimes striving to keep up as much as we are.

At other times, companions serve as the extra set of hands that The Doctor didn't know they needed. This comes into play in a few different ways.

Sometimes the companion is just in the right place at the right time, showing that The Doctor could not have been able to accomplish his mission on his own. In "Terror of the Autons," Jo is ordered to stay at UNIT headquarters in dismissive and arguably sexist fashion, but she sneaks away to help anyway, at one point giving a sly smile as she does so. When she pops up at just the right moment to help The Doctor, he yells at her for not staying behind, to which she replies, "It's a good thing for you that I didn't."

In "Genesis of the Daleks," The Fourth Doctor and his two companions Sarah Jane and Harry find themselves on a battle-field, during which The Doctor unwittingly steps on a land mine.

Luckily for him, Harry knows how to diffuse it, allowing The Doctor to live and the three of them to continue unharmed, for which The Doctor expresses thanks. While a minor point to the larger story, Harry's presence nevertheless becomes the difference that allows it to continue.

At times The Doctor finds themselves traveling with an intellectual equal, one able to keep up with his explanations with ease, who can formulate plans as well the Time Lord can, and who can match The Doctor's wit and humor quip for quip. We see this during "The Chase," where The First Doctor and his companions Ian, Barbara, and Vicki are running from time-traveling Daleks through multiple planets and historical periods. During these adventures, Ian shows himself to be an invaluable asset as he comes up with a trap for one of the Daleks, comes up with a theory about the supposedly haunted house they've stumbled into, and hatches a plan to steal the Daleks' time machine. It takes Ian time and effort to convince The Doctor to agree to this last one, but it ends up making a positive difference for the group.

Another example is Romana, a companion to The Fourth Doctor who also happens to be a fellow Time Lord. In "Destiny of the Daleks," she is regenerating, and decides upon the face of Princess Astra, whom actress Lalla Ward had played in the show previously. Not only does she take this form (against The Doctor's wishes at first), but she also chooses an outfit of long coat, high boots, and long scarf that looks very similar to The Doctor's chosen ensemble. As a fellow Time Lord, Romana is as smart and confident as The Doctor, able to understand his explanations and often clarifying or questioning them with her own knowledge and experience as well.

This companion trait overlaps with another, that being when one takes on the role of The Doctor's conscience, convincing him to choose an action that will be more compassionate. When The Tenth Doctor and Donna land on Pompeii the day before Vesuvius erupts, Donna wants to use this knowledge to help save the people of the city, which The Doctor refuses to the event's historical significance and inevitability. Donna nonetheless doesn't give up trying, eventually convincing him to save one family to whom they have become close over the course of the episode. After they drop the family off at a safe location far away from the burning city, The Doctor admits to Donna that he often needs someone to travel with him for this reason.

After The Eleventh Doctor regenerates into The Twelfth in "Deep Breath," Clara is first left trying to understand the concept of regeneration, much like Polly and Ben did when the First became the Second. After a resolution that saw a tentative relationship between the two, Clara receives a phone call from The Eleventh Doctor, first to assure her that everything is all right despite her reservations. But then he also asks her to help the new Doctor, describing him as being scared and trying to readjust to the universe after this latest change. He urges her to watch out for his new form, and to aid him as he tries to figure himself out. The Doctor needs a companion when he can't make sense of what's around him.

Sometimes the relationship between Doctor and companion takes on a romantic component. One of the first notable instances of this happens during the 1996 TV movie, where the newly regenerated Eighth Doctor falls in with a surgeon named Grace. As the two become closer, they are not only able to foil the evil intentions of The Master, but share a kiss as well.

One of the most significant relationships in this sense happened between The Tenth Doctor and Rose Tyler, which is hinted at during most of their time together. For the most part, The Doctor does not reciprocate any expressions of feelings that Rose shares with him, but when the two become separated at the end of "Doomsday," The Doctor silently grieves this loss, hinting that he may have felt more himself.

The Doctor's romantic connection to a companion takes on an entirely different dimension with the introduction of River Song, a mysterious scientist and traveler who first appears in "Silence in the Library." She hints to The Tenth Doctor that the two of them have a deep and meaningful history together, even though this is his first time meeting her. We learn much more about her after The Tenth Doctor regenerates into The Eleventh, as her story is greatly fleshed out over the course of the sixth season of the revived series, as she is revealed to be not only the daughter of The Doctor's other two companions, Amy Pond and Rory Williams, but also The Doctor's wife. River is a strong character able to match The Doctor's intellect much like Romana, which makes them a complementary fit for each other.

Finally, sometimes a companion's presence not only makes a difference when The Doctor is in a tough situation or when he needs to be challenged to show more sympathy for others, but takes on an extraordinary significance. When The Ninth Doctor is cornered by the Daleks, Rose is able to harness the power of the Time Vortex at the heart of the TARDIS in order to not only defeat their enemies, but to correct other fatal circumstances that they'd already caused as well. When The Eleventh Doctor faces a similar impossible situation at the hands of a group that wants to see all The Doctor's good deeds wiped from history, Clara jumps into The Doctor's time stream to become intertwined with every past incarnation's experience; to watch over them and save them from what the group wants to do. Sometimes companions take these extra-powerful steps in order to do what The Doctor themselves cannot do.

These are but a small portion of many instances showing how crucial companions are to The Doctor's life. They see The Doctor's actions in human terms, they provide extra help that The Doctor needs, they remind The Doctor of their mission to save others, they match wits with The Doctor when they need to, they show love for The Doctor and reveal him to be a caring being in a different way, and sometimes they go above and beyond to save not only The Doctor but the universe as well.

The Doctor often needs someone else to be with them, travel with them, point out blind spots, and take on what they can't do themselves. Just like any good companion would do.

PAUL'S COWORKERS

Paul mentions a number of other people with whom he works in his ministry. We are able to read a little more about some of them elsewhere in the New Testament, and others are little more than a name to the average reader, with little context or additional information about them. Both Paul and the communities to whom he wrote would have had a greater familiarity, which is why he often didn't feel the need to say much more about them.

This casual mentioning of names serves as another reminder that Paul's letters have a particularity to them. These writings are grounded in specific situations and relationships that were the real cause for their composition. Christian believers ascribe a timeless spiritual quality to them that often forgets that we're essentially reading somebody else's mail, and there are a set of unique factors that inform why Paul was writing to these communities or individuals.

The companions whom Paul mentions are quite numerous. Romans 16 alone includes thirty-five names of people to whom Paul wants to send his greetings, or who are currently traveling with Paul and whose well-wishes he wants to pass along. Some of these mentions include a brief recounting of why these people are important to him, and with others we are left to presume that the recipients of this letter know whom he is talking about.

Among those whom Paul talks about in his letters is a man named Barnabas. He is also mentioned in the book of Acts, introduced as a man named Joseph, given the surname Barnabas—meaning "son of encouragement"—as a descriptive title (Acts 4:36). After Paul's dramatic conversion experience on the road to Damascus in Acts 9, Barnabas is the one who presents him to the other apostles and helps make the case for his inclusion in their ministry (Acts 9:23–31). This begins a relationship where Barnabas is a mentor and teacher to Paul, as the two minister in Antioch for a year according to Acts 11, with Paul learning from Barnabas as much as he works alongside him.[1]

1. Spencer, "Barnabas," 399.

Paul writes about Barnabas at length in his letter to the Galatians, first summarizing a meeting that the two of them had with other prominent apostles in Jerusalem. They made their case for why they felt called to proclaim the gospel among the Gentiles while others were called to do so among Jewish believers, and the sides struck an accord that Paul and Barnabas's work was valid and good. However, in Galatians 2 Paul describes a dispute with Barnabas concerning the latter man's self-segregation from Gentiles during a meal, causing them to split for a time. However, the two seem to have made amends at some point, as Paul calls him a partner in 1 Corinthians 9:6.[2]

Paul also mentions a married couple several times, Aquila and Priscilla (sometimes called Prisca). They are introduced in Acts 18 as Jewish believers who had to flee Rome after the emperor ordered them to leave. They were tentmakers who welcomed Paul into their lives and business. Later in the same chapter, the three of them become partners in travel and evangelism to others.

Aquila and Priscilla seem to have an important ministry in their own right. At the end of Acts 18 they encounter a zealous, articulate believer named Apollos (who'd later become a frenemy of Paul), whom they pull aside to correct after they see him preaching the baptism of John the Baptist rather than focusing on Jesus (Acts 18:24–28). According to Paul, they had established a church in their home (1 Corinthians 16:19), and at some point "risked their necks" for him in an important way (Romans 16:3–5). All of this together shows Aquila and Priscilla as well-off, able to travel, courageous, and willing to teach others.[3]

Paul makes a brief reference to a woman named Chloe in 1 Corinthians 1, whose "people" have reported to him that the faith community there is experiencing divisions. This is the only mention of her name, although we can still make a few reasonable deductions. First, since she is listed as the head of household rather than a husband—the custom at the time—she likely would have

---

2. Spencer, "Barnabas," 398.

3. Spencer, "Aquila and Priscilla," 211.

had wealth, business connections, and people in her service.[4] As was possible with Aquila and Priscilla, she may have helped give financial support to Paul's ministry as was needed.

Both Acts and Paul's letters mention a man named Timothy, whom Paul has taken under his wing as an apprentice and ministry partner. Timothy is introduced in Acts 16 as already professing belief and discipleship. When Paul meets him, he has him circumcised in order to better fit in around the area, and takes him in as a fellow traveler and missionary.

Timothy appears to be one of Paul's closest companions and mentees. In Philippians 2:22, he describes their working relationship as being like a father with a son. Paul occasionally sends Timothy ahead of him or in his place to various communities, notably the Corinthians in particular, where he doesn't always seem to be received well. In 1 Corinthians 16:10, he encourages that community to be hospitable and kind toward him if he comes and stays with them. Paul mentions sending Timothy to the Thessalonians as well, although without such extra instructions to be nice to him (1 Thessalonians 3:2).

Paul sometimes names Timothy as a partner or brother, and he may even have coauthored some of the letters usually attributed to Paul. Timothy is mentioned at the beginning of Philippians, Colossians, and 1 and 2 Thessalonians, suggesting that he had a hand in composing these letters' contents. This, along with the instances when he sent Timothy ahead to various communities, shows the deep level of investment, trust, and love that Paul had for his protégé.

This is the smallest sample of names that Paul mentions in his letters, but as with The Doctor's various companions, each of these relationships had unique features, gifts, and showings of support. Barnabas began as a mentor for Paul as he came into his own as a missionary and apostle. Aquila and Priscilla were business partners, cotravelers, and capable evangelists in their own right. Chloe was a wealthy partner in ministry and possible benefactor. Timothy was a pupil, close friend, and colleague.

4. Thiselton, "Chloe," 594.

There are no instances where Paul insists upon his own capability independent of the help of others. He recognizes his need for the gifts, resources, encouragement, and accountability of the people around him. This in turn informs his passion for writing to these various Christian communities, which often include calling them to unity and mutual support even in the midst of their arguments and differences. While we may extrapolate general sentiments about community to be applied to our own settings from what he wrote, Paul's concern was for particular people to remain together. And, in part, it was because he had experienced the great value of companionship to his own life and ministry.

"YOU WERE RIGHT. SOMETIMES I NEED SOMEONE."

As shown in "The Waters of Mars," The Doctor tends to struggle with themselves when they travel alone. They are more easily distracted, they make decisions that can be short-sighted or ignore the greater ethical impact, they can become lost in their own thoughts, preoccupations, and loneliness, and they can act out in ways that are more hurtful than helpful.

There is still a risk of these things happening when The Doctor does have a companion, but it is much lower. Companions provide grounding for The Doctor; a second, third, or even fourth voice that gives additional perspective, clarity, and a sense of morality that keeps The Doctor from acting with a view of the situation that is too narrow, self-focused, or potentially dangerous. The Doctor has great knowledge, wisdom, and capability, but they still need help steering these gifts in the right direction.

Paul often admits that he is under no illusion that he can engage in mission and ministry by himself. The litany of names that he gives at the end of his letter to the Romans alone shows this. He may occasionally humble-brag in his letters about actions he's taken or about his background, but he has a well-developed sense of his dependence both on the grace of God and on the support of others for his work. Unlike with The Doctor, we are not offered much of a sense of what happens when Paul is left to his own devices, because he is often so quick to admit his shortcomings and his love and gratitude for those with whom he labors.

Years ago, I had waited until the last minute to file my taxes. I admit that it was pure sloth on my part that had led to this. I had made my appointment in early April, which led to a scrambling to ensure that I had the right amount owed lined up and ready to send in. The act of mailing it in was also last minute, literally, as that year I had to rush to the post office on the fifteenth to make sure that it would be postmarked and so that I could avoid any kind of penalty.

As you might be able to imagine, I was not the only one that day with such an issue. After waiting in line for a while as others in a similar predicament took care of their own business, I made it to the front and, to my relief, accomplished this important task and was able to head home more relaxed than when I'd entered.

At the same time that I was leaving the post office, another man who'd just completed his own filing was walking out as well. He was visibly agitated about having had to go through this process, and it included not only his having to rush to accomplish it but also the idea of doing it at all. I know this, because as we were leaving he turned to me and said, "What do you get for it?"

This interaction happened to fall on the same day as the 2013 Boston Marathon, when two bombs were detonated near the finish line, killing three people and injuring hundreds more. That day, I had watched both on TV and online as attendees rushed to safety, while others struggled to help those directly impacted by the explosions. I watched as first responders, charged with running toward tragedies rather than away from them, were assisting the injured, clearing paths for emergency vehicles, investigating what and who had caused it, and offering statements and instructions to inform the public of what was happening and the best ways that others could help.

People have a lot of different opinions and feelings about paying taxes. Many may feel similar to the gentleman with whom I was walking out of the post office that day. But the images from

Boston that day were, to me, the answer to "What do you get for it?" playing out in real time. At their best, such payments are an investment in community, in ways that maintain entities and institutions that benefit society at large. I personally may not always see or experience that benefit, but we are still able to be companions from afar to one another.

The Doctor sometimes needs help seeing what he gets for having a companion around. But in times when circumstances are most desperate and The Doctor is struggling to find the best way forward, the eyes, ears, hands, mind, and heart of a companion become invaluable. The Doctor invests in others by showing them just how big time and space is, giving them a larger perspective of the universe and adventures that show them a life beyond their existence on Earth. But as much as The Doctor knows, a companion will still help them see that same grand universe in a new way. Those times are when the benefit of The Doctor's investment in such relationships is clearest.

Paul cannot imagine the Christian life without such an investment. His sense of how God calls us to live as disciples of Jesus includes a call to live in community; to serve alongside others and invest in their well-being, regardless of whether one will always see what they'll get in return.

One of Paul's many encouragements to invest in others comes in Galatians 6:

> My friends, if anyone is detected in a transgression, you who have received the Spirit should restore such a one in a spirit of gentleness. Take care that you yourselves are not tempted. Bear one another's burdens, and in this way you will fulfill the law of Christ. For if those who are nothing think they are something, they deceive themselves. All must test their own work; then that work, rather than their neighbor's work, will become a cause for pride. For all must carry their own loads. Those who are taught the word must share in all good things with their teacher. Do not be deceived; God is not mocked, for you reap whatever you sow. If you sow to your own flesh, you will reap corruption from the flesh; but if you sow to

the Spirit, you will reap eternal life from the Spirit. So let us not grow weary in doing what is right, for we will reap at harvest-time, if we do not give up. So then, whenever we have an opportunity, let us work for the good of all, and especially for those of the family of faith. (Galatians 6:1–10)

In these few verses, Paul lists several important aspects of being in community with others. First, he mentions accountability, encouraging those who have transgressed either the larger group or something for themselves to be restored gently back into the community through a process of forgiveness and reformation.

Second, Paul encourages the Galatians to bear one another's burdens. Nobody should bear the brunt of their issues alone, and it becomes the calling of the community to ease that burden in loving and appropriate ways. In similar fashion, he encourages students and teachers to share in the joys that learning and mentoring brings. The common good of all, Paul writes in verse 10, should be the goal of the community

Finally, Paul includes a call to humility for individuals. In verses 3–4, he encourages people who are at risk of thinking too highly of themselves to perform a gut check. One's thoughts and work are not for self-glorification but for the good of all, and when one becomes too built up in their own mind, they can veer down a path that can be destructive for themselves or for others.

"Let us not grow weary in doing what is right," Paul writes. And what is right includes considering the impact of one's decisions on others. We can't always see this on our own—we may need the help of our companions to have a better grasp of what our choices could lead to. Likewise, we may be such a companion to someone else, the one who is entrusted to tell the truth or provide necessary resources so that others may thrive.

"You reap whatever you sow." Investing in others brings positive outcomes for everyone. What we get for being a companion depends on what we give. The Doctor articulates this at the end of "The Fires of Pompeii" when he admits to Donna that her presence is needed and welcome. His bringing her along has been for him as much as it was for her. He'd reaped what he had sown.

What we get for being in companionship with others is balance, perspective, and added clarity. And they receive the same from us.

9

Thank the Universe for Women

FOR MOST OF THE show's history, the main character of *Doctor Who* has been a man. For thirteen incarnations—the twelve Doctors from William Hartnell to Peter Capaldi, plus the War Doctor introduced for the fiftieth anniversary special—characters and viewers alike have been accustomed to The Doctor having one gender and race. On the show, people throughout the universe have either sought the "madman in a box" for help or trembled in fear at this same man's possible arrival to thwart plans or otherwise alter the accepted order of regimes.

And yet, as noted and explored in the previous chapter, many of The Doctor's companions and friends have been women, or otherwise female members of various species whom he has taken aboard. And while The Doctor is known through time and space as the one with power to change entire worlds, many women on the show have played pivotal roles themselves, either by assisting The Doctor with that effort or by redefining the past, present, or future by actions of their own.

As mentioned in the previous chapter, Rose Tyler reoriented the course of an important battle with the Daleks when she looked into the Time Vortex and used the power of the TARDIS coursing through her to single-handedly defeat their enemies, bring another character back to life, and scatter clues throughout time to help point The Doctor toward the key to winning this moment. In similar fashion, Clara Oswald jumped into The Eleventh Doctor's time stream to watch over him and save him from a threat on every life that he has lived.

Many of the most well-known, beloved, and consequential companions and friends of The Doctor have been women. Sarah Jane Smith was a committed and resourceful companion to The Third and Fourth Doctors and was one of the longest to travel with The Doctor. She eventually became an investigator of aliens in her own spinoff series and reappeared on the main show to help The Tenth Doctor as well. Romana, another companion of The Fourth Doctor, was also a fellow Time Lord who knew her way around the universe as well as he did. Aside from Rose and Clara in the revived series, Donna not only stands up to The Doctor when she believes he is not acting in good faith, but she even absorbs Time Lord capabilities for a brief time that proves pivotal to stopping a plot by Davros.

As mentioned in a previous chapter, a major shift took place on the show when a new mysterious character named Missy eventually revealed herself to be longtime nemesis The Master, regenerated for the first time as a woman. This particular incarnation brought a new dimension not only to the character, but to the dynamic between herself and The Doctor. Teasing and flirty, wicked and dangerous, Missy frequently dared those around her to underestimate her, and was just as full of surprises as previous incarnations of the character had been. This included giving the strongest possibility yet that The Master could be reformed, although The Twelfth Doctor's efforts were cut short by her own previous form.

River Song has been one of the most unique figures in recent *Doctor Who* lore. She first appears in the two-part story told in the episodes "Silence in the Library" and "Forest of the Dead," bumping into The Tenth Doctor and Donna in the universe's largest library with a group of archeological explorers. Upon discovering who The Doctor is, she begins dropping hints that they know each other, even though this is The Doctor's very first time meeting her.

To help prove that she's met him before, River produces a diary, the cover of which resembles the TARDIS, in which she has written of their adventures.

Since he is still not convinced as the situation becomes worse, River stands in close to him and whispers into his ear to prove how well they eventually know one another. The Doctor later reveals that she'd whispered his real name to him, and states that there's only one reason he'd ever tell someone his name. Unfortunately, River sacrifices herself before he can find out more about her.

River's story is fleshed out at length during The Eleventh Doctor's tenure. Every time she appears, The Doctor gets to know her more and more, while she on the other hand keeps producing the diary to ask what they have and haven't experienced together yet. "We keep meeting in the wrong order," he comments during "The Time of Angels," which brings him frustration while River greatly seems to enjoy the game.

As more and more information is revealed about who River is, we at least discover that she is knowledgeable, quick to think on her feet, and a capable fighter in combat. In "The Time of Angels" and "Flesh and Stone," it is revealed that she is a prisoner for killing someone, although we don't find out who for some time. Despite her incarceration, she is frequently able to escape, send messages to The Doctor in different ways, and as revealed in "The Husbands of River Song," she even sometimes steals the TARDIS without The Doctor's knowing.

During a season-long story, it is finally discovered that River is the daughter of one of The Doctor's companions and has Time Lord capabilities. She becomes a coveted prize of a religious order called The Silence, who hatch a plot to kill The Doctor, with River as the key player (The Doctor is her aforementioned victim that landed her in prison). After she initially foils their scheme, it causes a major upsetting of all of time, requiring The Doctor to take extensive measures to restore it. This includes marrying River during "The Wedding of River Song," in which River also confesses her deep love for him.

In "The Husbands of River Song," The Doctor has long been regenerated from Eleventh to Twelfth, and so it takes a good deal of the episode for River to realize who he is. By this point, she mentions that she's running out of room in her diary, which causes her to realize that her time with him must be ending in some way. At a pivotal moment in the episode, she confesses her frustration that she has never felt like The Doctor has loved her back, causing him to show her that he long has loved her as well. At the end of their adventure, The Doctor gives River her own sonic screwdriver, which will be the same one she uses in the library.

Given this description, it is obvious that River Song is not your typical companion. She matches wits with every version of The Doctor, and even knows her way around technology such as the TARDIS and the sonic screwdriver. She sometimes outwits him, she often acts independently of him, and yet she also carries a love for him that runs deeper than most other of The Doctor's fellow travelers and friends. Her life is intertwined with his in important and universe-altering ways.

In "The Doctor Falls," The Twelfth Doctor is having a conversation with Jon Simm's version of The Master after the latter character has become acquainted with his future self in Missy. He is dismayed by the direction that Missy seems to be headed, including her increasing displays of empathy. At one point, he asks The Doctor, "Is the future gonna be all girl?" The Doctor responds, "We can only hope."

This little bit of dialogue is a foreshadowing of The Doctor's own future. Upon realizing how close he is to regenerating, The Doctor initially refuses before finally giving in at the end of the next episode, "Twice upon a Time." After the usual fireworks that come with the regenerating moment, the new Doctor finds a mirror and discovers that, for the very first time, she has become a woman. Her reaction is to smile and say, "Oh, brilliant."

The Thirteenth Doctor, played by Jodie Whittaker, was naturally a sizable shift for the show, both onscreen and off. Fans who were used to a white man as The Doctor embraced the new possibilities, with many women and girls especially thankful for a new role model, while others insisted—and even after several seasons now, still insist—that what always was is what always should be, approaching this Doctor's tenure with an extra amount of skepticism and criticism.

For The Thirteenth Doctor's part on the actual show, she jumps—or in her first episode, falls—right into the action. After crashing through the roof of a train, she immediately hops up and uses an electrical cable to fend off a threatening alien presence that is terrorizing the passengers. Over the course of the rest of this episode, she builds a new sonic screwdriver, turns the main villain's weaponry against himself, and claims her identity as The Doctor.

The Doctor's new companions have little concept that she has been anything other than a woman. She does make reference to being a man previously and even forgets that she's now a woman at times, but as they have little concept of regeneration, they are slow to understand. Several characters who do know The Doctor nevertheless take time to become used to her new form as well. The director of MI-6 mistakes her companion Graham for The Doctor, saying he's read the file and that The Doctor is a man, to which the actual Doctor responds, "I've had an upgrade." A few episodes later, an old friend of The Ninth and Tenth Doctors, Captain Jack Harkness, also mistakes Graham for The Doctor. When Graham informs him that The Doctor is now a woman, Jack reacts with an impressed and knowing smile.

The tenure of The Thirteenth Doctor has been marked by adventure and detective work much like those before her. She shows a knack for building complex technological instruments out of whatever happens to be lying around, and a special empathy for her companions and for others, as well as an appreciation for historical figures such as Rosa Parks, Nicola Tesla, Mary Shelley, and Lord Byron. And yet she also stands toe to toe with the likes of the Daleks, Cybermen, and The Master as any Doctor ever has. The future is indeed all girl, and this Doctor has shown that to be a very good thing.

Doctor Who cannot be separated from its women characters. They are as crucial to what The Doctor identifies as needs in the universe as the central figure. And currently, they are one and the same. If women could not do what they are gifted to do on the show, then the universe would be in serious trouble.

And the same can be said for the church.

NOT SO SILENT AFTER ALL

Depending on the Christian circles you travel in, Paul does not always enjoy a very positive reputation when it comes to the role of women. Several passages in the New Testament, whether in letters that can be directly traced back to him or in letters written by other followers yet with his name on them, seem to severely limit the role of women in the church, in marriage, or in life in general.

Paul deserves a bit of reclamation on this point, because this reputation is not fully earned. His genuine letters point to an apostle who welcomes the involvement and ministry of women without much qualification or limitation. And when put up against other passages stamped with his name, we see a stark contrast between what Paul really envisioned for women in the communities to which he wrote versus what subsequent generations of followers wanted women to do, or not do.

First, because I've introduced the concept, it would be responsible to say a little more about "genuine Paul" as opposed to these later followers.

Many biblical scholars argue that several letters in the New Testament that are attributed to Paul may not have originated from his hand. The clearest consensus regarding this is for what are commonly called the Pastoral Epistles: 1 Timothy, 2 Timothy, and Titus. These three have been dated to several decades after Paul's death, and utilize a different writing style and vocabulary than those letters deemed authentic to Paul. They also signal a shift in theology, as many of Paul's letters operate with the expectation that Jesus is due to return very soon, whereas these three letters expound upon good church organization and management, without that sense of urgency.

Ephesians, Colossians, and 2 Thessalonians have scholars more split as to whether they came directly from Paul or not. There are still some shifts in language and theology present, but they don't seem as far removed as the Pastoral Epistles. It may have been that immediate followers of Paul, with his thought and ideas fresh in their minds yet also with an eye toward becoming more assimilated to larger cultural ideas, wrote them.

One final note: why would people write letters like these and then put someone else's name at the top? Borg and Crossan note that this was actually quite a common practice in that time, and would not have seemed unusual then.[1] If undertaken today, many would raise accusations of forgery, but back then it was to give additional authority or to further a school of thought.

So with that extended preface, Paul is not yet out of the woods when it comes to what he may or may not have thought about women. Even if we can set aside some letters as not being directly from his views on the matter, we still need to ask about Paul's vision for this burgeoning Jesus-centered movement that he was helping to organize.

One of the best places to start might be in 1 Corinthians 14:

> What should be done then, my friends? When you come together, each one has a hymn, a lesson, a revelation, a tongue, or an interpretation. Let all things be done for building up. If anyone speaks in a tongue, let there be only two or at most three, and each in turn; and let one interpret. But if there is no one to interpret, let them be silent in church and speak to themselves and to God. Let two or three prophets speak, and let the others weigh what is said. If a revelation is made to someone else sitting nearby, let the first person be silent. For you can all prophesy one by one, so that all may learn and all be encouraged. And the spirits of prophets are subject to the prophets, for God is a God not of disorder but of peace. (As in all the churches of the saints,
> *women should be silent in the churches. For they are not permitted to speak, but should be subordinate, as the*

1. Borg and Crossan, *First Paul*, 14.

law also says. If there is anything they desire to know, let them ask their husbands at home. For it is shameful for a woman to speak in church.

Or did the word of God originate with you? Or are you the only ones it has reached?) Anyone who claims to be a prophet, or to have spiritual powers, must acknowledge that what I am writing to you is a command of the Lord. Anyone who does not recognize this is not to be recognized. So, my friends, be eager to prophesy, and do not forbid speaking in tongues; but all things should be done decently and in order. (1 Corinthians 14:26–40, italics mine)

The emphasized section of this passage seems to indicate that Paul prefers for women not to have a speaking role in the church. And, in fact, some corners of Christianity today use this passage to argue that specific point. But it may not be that simple.

There is a good chance that verses 33–36 are a later addition by an editor, perhaps for another time, place, and situation. One reason for this is that the larger argument that Paul is making in 1 Corinthians 14 is about disorder in worship, particularly concerning the use of prophecy and speaking in tongues. He is arguing that there is a proper and orderly way for people to share these gifts, as he proposes limits on how many may share them, and only if there is someone present with the gift of interpretation.

In this context, verses 33–36 read like an interruption; a strange change of subject that strains to fit the points about silence and order. If these verses were removed, this part of the letter would have a much smoother reading.

A larger concern about these verses is how they seem to go against how Paul speaks of women elsewhere, both in 1 Corinthians and in other letters. And here begins our larger consideration of how Paul really valued women in his life and ministry.

First, in 1 Corinthians 11, Paul gives some other instructions to both men and women about worship, particularly about hair and head coverings:

Any man who prays or prophesies with something on his head disgraces his head, but any woman who prays or prophesies with her head unveiled disgraces her head—it is one and the same thing as having her head shaved. For if a woman will not veil herself, then she should cut off her hair; but if it is disgraceful for a woman to have her hair cut off or to be shaved, she should wear a veil. For a man ought not to have his head veiled, since he is the image and reflection of God; but woman is the reflection of man. Indeed, man was not made from woman, but woman from man. Neither was man created for the sake of woman, but woman for the sake of man. For this reason a woman ought to have a symbol of authority on her head, because of the angels. Nevertheless, in the Lord woman is not independent of man or man independent of woman. For just as woman came from man, so man comes through woman; but all things come from God. Judge for yourselves: is it proper for a woman to pray to God with her head unveiled? Does not nature itself teach you that if a man wears long hair, it is degrading to him, but if a woman has long hair, it is her glory? For her hair is given to her for a covering. But if anyone is disposed to be contentious—we have no such custom, nor do the churches of God. (1 Corinthians 11:4–16)

Paul is very concerned about proper showings of humility and etiquette, illustrating that arguments about the proper way to behave in church date back to its earliest days of organization.

Aside from that, however, if we pay attention to the subtext of Paul's instructions to women in this passage, one thing that we notice is this: women are sharing prophesies during public worship. They are openly using their spiritual gifts to speak a word from God, and Paul and others seem to treat it as a natural, wonderful, appropriate, and needed contribution to their gatherings. Paul may be overly concerned about the state of one's head while doing it, but here he does not treat women prophesying as something to be silenced. As with 1 Corinthians 14, he would just prefer that one—man or woman—do it according to a certain level of self-awareness and decorum, to ensure that the community's gatherings have some structure and order to them.

Furthermore, Paul argues in this passage that men and women belong to each other. He first notes that "woman came from man," a nod to the story of Adam and Eve in Genesis 2–3, but later states that both man comes from woman and woman from man, and neither should be independent of the other. In fact, Paul quickly adds that all of us, no matter our gender, come from God. There are influences of patriarchy in Paul's thinking, but he tempers it with a healthy dose of recognition that each needs the other, and may benefit from the gifts of the other.

Perhaps the clearest sense that we may get regarding Paul's valuing of women in the church is in how often he mentions women as partners in his ministry.

In Romans 16:1–2, Paul commends a woman named Phoebe, whom he identifies as a deacon at a church in Cenchreae. The word "deacon" may also be translated "minister," suggesting that she was active in ministering in that community. Not only that, but Paul offers gratitude to her as a financial patron of his ministry as well.

A few verses later in 16:7, Paul commends a man and woman named Andronicus and Junia, whom he names as family. At some point, they were prisoners together, which was probably a harrowing shared experience in itself. But then Paul names them as "prominent among the apostles." Junia, a woman, is given the title apostle by Paul without hedging and with great affection for her partnership.

Romans 16 mentions a number of other women, either by name or relationship, whom Paul greets and thanks for their work in the church. They seem to be doing much more than preparing funeral dinners and leading the ladies' tea. These activities may have had value both past and present, but these mentions suggest that they are right in the thick of organizing, teaching, evangelizing, prophesying, and so much more in this new movement. Paul is encouraging them rather than trying to reign them in, because he knows what their gifts contribute to their mission and ministry together.

Paul expresses admiration and gratitude to many woman companions for doing what they could to benefit the church. This avalanche of names and thank-yous suggests that he wants them to do anything but be silent, lest everyone else miss out on what God has given them to share.

BEYOND GENDER FENCES

The previous discussion of Paul's view of women may be a relief to some, and unconvincing to others. After all, those Pastoral Epistles are still part of the New Testament, and are used by many a Christian institution as a user's manual for how to organize their leadership, teaching, and preaching structures in what they see as a faithfully "biblical" way. Women are relegated to certain roles and banned from others, all in the name of what these places believe is according to God's plan for humanity, as proposed in these letters that have been elevated to scriptural status, far beyond their original intended purpose to advise or instruct particular faith communities at certain points in their collective lives.

Even what are considered the authentic letters of Paul may still present issues for individuals or groups seeking guidance, affirmation, or boundaries for how to live. We may be able to explain, or at least hypothesize, about the circumstances surrounding a text like 1 Corinthians 14:33–36, but its presence may still be troubling for many, regardless of authorship or intention.

In her book *A Year of Biblical Womanhood*, Rachel Held Evans writes:

> Among the women praised in Scripture are warriors, widows, slaves, sister wives, apostles, teachers, concubines, queens, foreigners, prostitutes, prophets, mothers, and martyrs. What makes these women's stories leap from the page is not the fact that they all conform to some kind of universal ideal, but that, regardless of the culture or context in which they found themselves, they lived their lives with valor. They lived their lives with faith. As much as we may long for the simplicity of a single definition of "biblical womanhood," there is no one right way to be a woman, no mold into which we must each cram ourselves—not if Deborah, Ruth, Rachel, Tamar, Vashti,

Esther, Priscilla, Mary Magdalene, and Tabitha have anything to say about it.[2]

There is a case to be made that the words attributed to Paul in texts like 1 Corinthians 14:33–36 and the Pastoral Letters are not actually his ideas about how to organize worship gatherings and other church activities. The strongest argument against it is how much affection and gratitude he has for women like Chloe, Phoebe, Junia, Priscilla, Euodia, Syntyche, and Apphia, along with other unnamed grandmothers, mothers, and sisters at the end of Romans. He calls women like these fellow workers, deacons, apostles, and benefactors, and implies that they share in his work either in hands-on ways or through financial or prayerful support. If it wasn't for them, the ministry that they share would not be as strong.

There are words in some New Testament letters that seem to forbid women from some of the very work that Paul celebrates these particular women doing. That he so strongly commends so many for their efforts and gifts would greatly tip the scales toward his appreciation of women being their full, authentic, and gifted selves for God and for others, to the chagrin of at least some of his later followers. But to Paul himself, women were essential to the life of community discipleship.

In much the same way, it could be argued that if it weren't for women, The Doctor would often be lost. Their gifts and insights often make the difference between an adventure being cut short, or reaching a positive conclusion. At various times, women with whom The Doctor travels provide empathy or gentleness to balance The Doctor's gruff or overly analytical manner. At times, they are able to charm someone into providing information after The Doctor has quickly alienated someone with too direct an approach. At times, they remind The Doctor that their nature is to save people rather than abandon them. At times, they use skills from their career to help others caught in the crosshairs of battle.

2. Evans, *Year of Biblical Womanhood*, 295.

At times, they remind The Doctor that they are worthy of love and are in need of care just like anyone else.

The Doctor often embraces these contributions eventually, if not immediately. As explored in the chapter about companions, The Doctor recognizes how much they need someone else to accompany them, not just to temper loneliness but because their perspective and talents often add something critical to the help that they provide to the universe. And The Doctor pays no mind whether those who accompany them are men, women, or even human. This is a signal of The Doctor's appreciation of diversity across galaxies without regard to preapproved worth or boundaries.

The Doctor tends to judge the people and aliens they meet according to their specific actions rather than according to notions of species or gender beforehand. Paul seems to do the same thing, often celebrating men and women with whom he works because he's seen what they've done and he's received their help and love. When these particular people and actions are placed on one side of a scale against a handful of Bible verses, they will weigh much more every time.

The church and the world have received the gifts of countless women, some known and many unknown. Along with the women highlighted by Paul and Rachel Held Evans already, we could also lift up the likes of the desert mothers, Catherine of Siena, Teresa of Avila, Clare of Assisi, Mother Teresa, Sojourner Truth, Antoinette Brown, Marian Wright Edelman, and Coretta Scott King, among so many others whose passion and talents have helped form the way people of faith gather in community, organize to pursue justice, and approach preaching and worship.

Had these women remained silent, the church and the world would have missed out on the authentic movement of God's Spirit in their lives. We may be able to name women in our own lives who have shaped our lives and our faith, who have been the difference between one life path and another, whose not remaining silent has been a gift to who we have been and who we have become.

God seems to care less about gender qualifications than many humans do. Paul, The Doctor, and history have shown that life-shaping gifts have little regard for our rules as to whom they should be bestowed. Instead, God is more concerned with whether we acknowledge, receive, and celebrate them, along with those to whom they are given.

10

Regenerating Hope

ONE OF THE SPECIAL qualities of being a Time Lord is the fact that, once they meet a fatal situation, they are able to regenerate rather than die. Just before he regenerates, The Ninth Doctor describes it as "this little trick, this little way of cheating death."

In the mythology of the show, regeneration features several things. First, they take on a new form, usually also with new mannerisms (the natural side effect of another actor making the role their own).

Second, they are only afforded so many of these: various points in the show say that members of this species get twelve, and that's it. However, the show has also found ways to side-step this rule for both The Doctor and The Master when it has been deemed suitable, so this isn't the most critical feature in Time Lords enjoying such a benefit.

Whenever The Doctor regenerates into a new form, it is usually presented as a jarring experience for all involved. This includes not just The Doctor him—or herself, who most directly is affected by the change, but also others around them in different ways. This makes sense, since regeneration involves The Doctor's cells and molecules reconfiguring from old to new. The process of changing from one form to another involves pain and adjustment in more than one sense, not all of them merely physical in nature.

Regeneration affords The Doctor a new life after a former one has come to an end. As many times as it has happened, it is always a monumental event; one that is pivotal for The Doctor and surrounding characters that bring consequences that are joyful, exciting, disorienting, hopeful, and sad all at the same time.

The actual process of regeneration has not been presented as having a set amount of time in which it happens. Over the course of "The Tenth Planet," The First Doctor hints at feeling tired and unwell, and at the end of the episode collapses in the control room of the TARDIS. His body morphs into that of The Second Doctor, and during the next series, "The Power of the Daleks," The Second Doctor seems not to suffer any aftereffects, immediately jumping into a new adventure without any physical hindrance.

We may hold this in contrast with later regenerations, such as when The Ninth Doctor becomes The Tenth. All seems well at the end of "The Parting of the Ways," when The Tenth Doctor immediately suggests that he and Rose travel to a new planet. At the beginning of his first full episode, "The Christmas Invasion," he collapses and spends a sizable amount of time passed out as his body finishes the cycle.

Something similar happens after The Eleventh Doctor becomes The Twelfth. After abruptly taking on his new face and rushing to steer an out of control TARDIS to safety, he collapses and needs to be cared for by Clara and other friends until his new form stabilizes. When The Twelfth Doctor suffers a blow that assures his regeneration into The Thirteenth, it takes him several episodes to give in completely and allow himself to be transformed. There is no set time frame for the process.

One recurring feature of regeneration seems to be its effect on the new Doctor's memory. As their body adjusts to a new form, so must their mind. After The Second Doctor's regeneration, there are several points in "The Power of the Daleks" when he speaks of his former self in the third person: at one point, he asks his companion Polly, "The Doctor kept a diary, didn't he?" In the 1996 movie, The Eighth Doctor agonizes over not being able to remember who he is. The Thirteenth Doctor can remember some details of her identity after her regeneration, such as her previous incarnation being a white-haired Scotsman and that she never refuses when somebody asks her for help. But it is only much later in "The Woman Who Fell to Earth" that she fully regains her sense of who she is.

Sometimes regeneration energy can be used for more than just beginning a new life. It can also be lent to others, used to heal, or used to destroy. At the end of "The Christmas Invasion," The Tenth Doctor has his hand cut off during a fight and is able to materialize a new one before his regeneration cycle completes. While The Twelfth Doctor is still in the early stages of his regenerating, he allows energy to explode out of him to defeat a threat from the Cybermen in "The Doctor Falls." In "Let's Kill Hitler," the partial Time Lord River Song sacrifices her remaining regenerations in order to revive a dying Eleventh Doctor.

The Doctor does not always welcome their regeneration with happiness. When the Time Lords put The Second Doctor on trial during "The War Games," one of their punishments is that he will be forced to take a new form. He protests their decision, including the choice of possible faces that they present to him. He yells his objections as the process begins, and it is our final glimpse of The Doctor in this form until he returns in special episodes later.

The Tenth Doctor is given a prophecy that the end of his life is coming, and he tries to run from it as best he can. In "The End of Time," he finally realizes that he can't avoid it any longer and grieves before it happens. He takes time to say goodbye to every character who has ever been his companion, and his final words are "I don't want to go."

As mentioned earlier, The Twelfth Doctor also greets his impending regeneration with great difficulty. He tries to hide the glow of energy emanating from his fingers, and objects loudly during the final moments of "The Doctor Falls" that he doesn't want to change any more. He further resists the change during most of "Twice Upon a Time." When he does finally decide to give in to the process, he gives advice to his future self before completely letting go and allowing the transformation to happen.

In "The Woman Who Fell to Earth," The Thirteenth Doctor gives some insight as to why regeneration is not always something that her past selves have embraced. She describes the process has first having a "moment where you're sure you're about to die, and then you're born." The word she uses to describe it is terrifying, suggesting that Time Lords still experience everything of death despite what happens after.

As much as The Doctor sometimes has trouble accepting the changes that come with regeneration, the characters closest to them also go through a time of grieving and adjustment. Polly and Jamie repeatedly wonder whether The Second Doctor really is the same person, observing that he talks and acts completely different from The First Doctor whom they had come to know. When River meets The Tenth Doctor, she makes a comment during "Forest of the Dead" that he is not "her Doctor," alluding to the fact that she is much better acquainted with him in other forms. When he objects, saying that he is in fact The Doctor, she replies, "Not yet." After The Eleventh Doctor has become The Twelfth in "Deep Breath," Clara struggles to understand what has happened and asks other characters who know him to help her change him back. It is only after she gets a phone call from The Doctor whom she knows better, imploring her to help his regenerated form, that she begins to accept what has happened.

Perhaps related to The Doctor's mixed feelings on the process of regeneration is that they never use this feature of themselves as a crutch or fallback. They confront danger to overcome it and to save others, but also with the intent of getting out of it alive themselves rather than resting on the possibility of regeneration to get them out of a tight spot. The Doctor chooses to live another day whenever possible; to make the most out of every life that they've been given, receiving them all as a precious gift to be used wisely for exploring the universe and helping people. Regeneration presents an opportunity to start again, but The Doctor never rushes to do so.

For The Doctor, the process of becoming something new is complex. It involves the death of what has been, and the hesitant embrace of what has begun. Despite that hope of the new, it can take a lot of time for The Doctor and others to see and receive and live into that hope themselves.

A SPIRITUAL BODY

Paul spends most of chapter 15 of 1 Corinthians discussing his thoughts on the resurrection. His initial words on the matter seem to stem from yet another dispute that he is having with this particular community.

In the first few verses, Paul reminds the Corinthians of the message that he passed on to them, which he had received from others. This includes his own experience of the risen Christ, which set him on this new path of proclaiming God's grace to the Gentiles. This experience of God's grace—God's presence and love, which God initiated and which Paul accepted and allowed to change him—spurred him on to proclaim and continue what others before him began via their own visions of resurrection.

After this opening, Paul focuses on people within the Corinthian church who dispute that Jesus was actually raised from the dead. For Paul, Jesus being raised is the cornerstone of much of what he has been proclaiming. Not only that, but it is a foundational claim of the entire movement. Without Jesus being raised, nobody else is raised, either. And if there is no resurrection, then this entire enterprise of believing is for nothing (1 Corinthians 15:12–19).

Paul also contends with an apparent issue that a lack of belief in the resurrection seems to be influencing people's behavior for the worse. Or, alternatively, holding a belief in the resurrection is not influencing behavior for the better. If there is no resurrection, then there is no reason to be transformed in heart, mind, and action. He offers a mocking quote that has become reflected in some of the Corinthians' actions: "Let us eat and drink, for tomorrow we die (1 Corinthians 15:32)." This attitude does not represent the life-changing effect that God raising the principal figure of their movement is meant to have on them.[1]

In terms of Paul's actual theology of resurrection—what he believes it signifies and how it works—he fleshes that out in the latter half of the chapter. He seemed to want to address the Corinthians' mistaken notions about its effects before exploring what it says about God, Jesus, and humanity in wider and deeper ways.

Since some are denying the veracity of the resurrection, Paul first shares some thoughts on how be believes it happens:

> But someone will ask, "How are the dead raised? With what kind of body do they come?" Fool! What you sow does not come to life unless it dies. And as for what you sow, you do not sow the body that is to be, but a bare seed, perhaps of wheat or of some other grain. But God gives it a body as he has chosen, and to each kind of seed its own body. Not all flesh is alike, but there is one flesh for human beings, another for animals, another for birds, and another for fish. There are both heavenly bodies and earthly bodies, but the glory of the heavenly is one thing, and that of the earthly is another. There is one glory of the sun, and another glory of the moon, and another glory of the stars; indeed, star differs from star in glory. So it is with the resurrection of the dead. What is sown is perishable, what is raised is imperishable. It is sown in dishonor, it is raised in glory. It is sown in weakness, it is raised in power. It is sown a physical body, it is raised a spiritual body. If there is a physical body, there is also a spiritual body. Thus it is written, "The first man, Adam, became a living being"; the last Adam became a life-giving spirit. But it is not the spiritual that is first, but the physical, and then the spiritual. The first man was from the earth, a man of dust; the second man is from heaven. As was the man of dust, so are those who are of the dust; and as is the man of heaven, so are those who are of heaven. Just as we have borne the image of the man of dust, we will also bear the image of the man of heaven. What I am saying, brothers and sisters, is this:

1. I reflect more on this part of 1 Corinthians 15 in *Wonder and Whiskey: Insights on Faith from the Music of Dave Matthews Band* (Wipf & Stock, 2018).

115

flesh and blood cannot inherit the kingdom of God, nor does the perishable inherit the imperishable. (1 Corinthians 15:35–50)

Paul uses a seed and plant metaphor to make his case for how resurrection works. In planting a seed, the hope is that with certain conditions and resources that seed will give way to and produce a flower, a tree, a vegetable, grain, or whatever else it is the particular seed for. Every seed is different in this regard, just as people, animals, birds, and fish all have different kinds of physical bodies.

And yet what is sowed is not what is reaped. When one plants a seed, it may be for a certain type of plant, but it is not the seed itself that sprouts from the ground. Instead, the seed gives way to something else. Through growth and transformation, the seed that is sown is reaped as whatever type of plant it is a seed for. The seed becomes the plant, and this is considered its completed state; what it aspires to become.[2]

In much the same way, Paul argues, people are sown in a physical body, but through a process of change initiated by God, we are reaped as a spiritual body in the resurrection. The physical body, according to Paul, has certain characteristics: perishability, dishonor, and weakness. Likewise, the new spiritual body brought about through resurrection has certain characteristics: imperishability, glory, and power.

One important element to note about Paul's views on resurrection here is how important it is to Paul that one still has a body after the resurrection. The term "spiritual body" may seem like a contradiction: is it a spirit, or is it a body? For Paul, the answer is both. In the resurrection, one still takes on a form like that of our earthly selves, but with none of the characteristics that cause it to wear out or break down. The spiritual body is beyond that temporal quality, made instead of the stuff of heaven itself.

Paul has one additional piece of his argument to make, which ties resurrection to a future hope:

2. Sampley, "First Letter to the Corinthians," 987.

Listen, I will tell you a mystery! We will not all die, but we will all be changed, in a moment, in the twinkling of an eye, at the last trumpet. For the trumpet will sound, and the dead will be raised imperishable, and we will be changed. For this perishable body must put on imperishability, and this mortal body must put on immortality. When this perishable body puts on imperishability, and this mortal body puts on immortality, then the saying that is written will be fulfilled: "Death has been swallowed up in victory." "Where, O death, is your victory? Where, O death, is your sting?" The sting of death is sin, and the power of sin is the law. But thanks be to God, who gives us the victory through our Lord Jesus Christ. Therefore, my beloved, be steadfast, immovable, always excelling in the work of the Lord, because you know that in the Lord your labor is not in vain. (1 Corinthians 15:51–58)

Much of what Paul writes in his letters is tied to his belief that Jesus' return and God's great cleanup of heaven and Earth is about to happen at any time. It's why he advises against getting too comfortable or becoming too bogged down in certain earthly concerns. Instead, his letters are fueled by a certain vigilance for what God is about to do.

As he concludes a long section on the resurrection, he ties it in more directly to this vigilance. Before even everyone he is writing to dies, all will be changed into this new spiritual form. And it will happen at a moment's notice when the last trumpet sounds. That moment of change, brought about by God's decisive action to reform and renew the world, will also signify a final victory over sin and death. There will be no more perishability, suffering, or imperfection when all this happens. Instead, all will become a part of a new resurrected form of reality, of which our spiritual bodies will be a part.

In this passage, Paul places his hope in what God is about to do, one a smaller version of a larger event. For those who die, God will redeem them in resurrected forms that will not be able to die again. Jesus' own resurrection was the first sign of what is to come in this regard; what Paul calls the "first fruit" of what will follow as others who have been sown will eventually be reaped. And this is a particular sign of the greater process of transformation that God is bringing into existence for all of creation, where all death and suffering will end and a permanent glorious reality will take its place.

Paul wishes this hope for the Corinthians: that it will inspire and influence their thoughts and deeds as they seek to live together in community. He wishes for them to live in hope for their own resurrection, but also watchful for the bigger wonderful things that God is bringing and will bring for all.

BUT WE WILL ALL BE CHANGED

Regeneration and resurrection are not the same thing. That is where we should start this part of the chapter. There are a few qualities that differentiate one from the other.

First, the source of each differs. In *Doctor Who*, Time Lords have harnessed the power of the Time Vortex for their own means, which has led to their being able to regenerate into a new form. This power is something that they have taken for their own use, and exploited or appropriated to suit their own ends. Regeneration is something that The Doctor and others have given themselves.

The source of resurrection is the power of God, a gift that God chooses to share with Jesus and humanity. When Paul and other Biblical writers reference the resurrection, the phrasing that they often use is that God raised Jesus, or Jesus was raised by God. They are often careful to state that God is the one that makes resurrection possible, first for Jesus and then also for others. People do not will their own resurrection, nor can they contain God's power to use for their own ends. Instead, God shares this life-giving gift, and others are able to receive it.

Second, regeneration is an event that happens over and over. A Time Lord may receive a new body and another lifetime, but both still have an end date that triggers another cycle until one has used up all twelve (except, as mentioned, in special cases like The

Doctor and The Master). Regeneration still has an expiration date, even if it's further into the future than it is for any human being.

Resurrection is a one-time event, because its recipient only needs one. In the words of Paul shared earlier in this chapter, "When this perishable body puts on imperishability, and this mortal body puts on immortality, then the saying that is written will be fulfilled: 'Death has been swallowed up in victory'" (1 Corinthians 15:54). Unlike with regeneration, the new body that one is given in resurrection will not wear out again. Its effects are everlasting.

This is not to say that we are unable to also find similarities between the two. Both, for instance, are quite disorienting for people who experience them, either directly or indirectly. Some companions have a very difficult time accepting that The Doctor in their new form is still somehow the same person that they knew before. Regeneration brings about a new, strange, unfamiliar reality for those unaccustomed to it, and it takes them time to adjust before they can experience anything resembling joy or relief.

If we venture outside Paul's letters, we can see this at work for those who first encounter Jesus after he is raised in the Gospels. Some disciples doubt even after seeing him at the end of Matthew (28:17); in the original ending of Mark, the women run away without telling anyone (16:8); the disciples don't believe the women when they first share the news in Luke (24:11); and Thomas holds out accepting the news until he can see for himself in John (20:25).

But in the case of the Corinthians, the issue of not believing in the truth of the resurrection is why Paul writes about it in chapter 15 to begin with. The first part of this chapter concerns the domino effect caused by saying that God did not raise Jesus: that means that nobody else will be raised either, and all our faith is in vain. In another letter, he also needs to reassure the Thessalonians of what resurrection will mean for them and for their loved ones who have already died (1 Thessalonians 4:13–18). Even for those who have accepted the news, these words may be needed for further reassurance, especially in times of difficulty and doubt. Accepting it may take time, even among those initially more willing to believe.

The hope and reassurance that both regeneration and resurrection brings is perhaps the most important similarity between them. Even as jarring and upsetting as regeneration may be, The Doctor always finds their footing again. In her description of what the process is like, The Thirteenth Doctor does include that it still involves death and a feeling of terror, but after that, she describes hearing echoes of who she was but also a call toward who she is. That time of reconciling the two may take time and be disorienting at first, but each time it eventually brings both The Doctor and their companions into a renewed sense of purpose and excitement for the continued adventures that they may have around the universe.

"The last enemy to be destroyed is death," Paul writes. And he acknowledges that some among the believers have or will have already experienced it. But he always brings a future hope to his writing that eventually all will be renewed and the same gift that God shared with Jesus will be shared with all.

This may be most important for Paul's audience to hear as they continue to struggle against the earthly powers that seem to be working against them: infighting, disputes over theology or sharing of resources, pressures from outside groups and the empire of the day, and quotidian concerns like caring for a household and maintaining a work life. They may be looking not only toward the same future that Paul envisions, but they also may be looking for signs of resurrection sooner than that, asking how God may be making all things new even before that great day that they are expecting.

"Life depends on change and renewal," The Second Doctor says to his companions as they still struggle to understand his regeneration. There is a hope in such change and renewal that Paul's communities and modern believers may maintain in the present time, even as one waits for something greater to happen in the future. Resurrection may have a great impact on how we live, which is part of Paul's message to the Corinthians: change and renewal is for our outlook, our behavior, and our interactions with others in the here and now.

I am writing this chapter as concerns about the novel coronavirus have the world deeply shaken. Many elements of society have been shut down to help keep it from spreading further, and many people are scared and anxious, wondering what this will mean both short-term and long-term, how best to be safe, and how long this will last. Many of the closings and increased caution began to ramp up just before the celebration of Easter, leading many to wonder whether or how we could celebrate resurrection when much of the world will still be experiencing death and despair.

This same time has also featured an increase in people reaching out to one another. It has featured people checking in to others' emotional and spiritual needs, as well as to physical needs for those with more limited means. It has featured a certain flourishing of art, as museums, authors, musicians, and other artists have shared their work freely to help provide encouragement. It has featured people being given relief—albeit mostly temporary—from financial burdens such as loans, bills, and other expenses.

These are signs of resurrection hope showing up in a moment where people are desperate to receive them. It may not yet be the fulfillment of all that people wish for, but glimpses may still be found to carry us through to a new day.

Even if this wasn't happening and people were experiencing something closer to what we may consider normal, one may be able to find such hope through kindness, art, service, and relief. These serve as signs of God making things new in the midst of doubt, sadness, and uncertainty, providing the change and renewal upon which life depends.

Afterword

AROUND THE TIME THAT Jodie Whittaker was announced as The Thirteenth Doctor, I developed a theory about fandom that seems to hold true in the majority of circumstances. Whittaker was, predictably, not well received by all corners of the *Doctor Who* fanbase. Not everyone was happy with the fact that for the first time in the show's history The Doctor would be a woman. It was too big of a change, *too female of a change*, for some to handle.

At the same time, so many women and girls were thrilled with the change. They finally had a Doctor who was more like them; who'd be more relatable than previous ones had been.

I've mentioned that fans of the show have their favorite Doctors. For some it's the one they first encountered when they discovered the show, the one who served as their introduction to the *Doctor Who* universe. For others it may have to do with the one they knew best during a formative or transitional time: The Doctor you watched as a child or teenager or young adult may have special meaning for you because the show was an anchor as you got to know yourself in a certain season of life. And for still others, your favorite Doctor might be the one whose style or personality is most attractive because you find it relatable or different or needed for your own reasons.

All of this is to say that one's favorite Doctor or Doctors are the ones who provided the most accessible entry into all that the show has to offer. It's as much dependent on your own life circumstances as it is the decisions that the showrunner makes.

Afterword

This is not necessarily a new or unique theory. You could apply it to any other form of art, a certain era of your favorite sports team, or other brands that you follow. Your favorite music might be what got you through high school. Your favorite baseball team might have been a perpetual bottom-dweller when you were in your twenties, but you still appreciate them at that stage because you have fond memories of listening to games with a parent on the radio.

This theory may apply to faith as well. As a pastor, I have years of firsthand experience navigating the treasured songs and traditions of congregations, who usually don't just love them for their own sake but because they represent years of memories. When people hear certain Scripture passages or pieces of music, they may be taken back to people and places they associate with them, for better or worse.

The letters of Paul are a unique example of this theory at work. His words have given so much life and foundation to Christian faith, discipleship, and the church over the centuries. They have spanned the world over and over again, influencing entire movements of thought and action, all the way to present day.

As with other parts of the Bible, Paul may be the first to whom one may turn for words of comfort, assurance, and insight. They may be the words best remembered from pivotal moments, his thoughts being the ones that came at just the right time.

But many others may prefer to keep their distance from Paul because his words have been used to cause damage and harm rather than provide encouragement. As many stories of hope may be shared regarding his letters, there are just as many where his words have inspired people to leave him, the Bible, the church, or faith itself behind.

Sometimes this theory can work the other way, too.

As we have made it to the end of this exploration of seeing where The Doctor and Paul merge and diverge, I do not expect that, if you fall into the latter category regarding Paul in particular, I have been the one who has fully persuaded you to give him another chance. But I did write this in the hope that it will offer you a new access point to his life and ideas.

Paul believed that he was called to proclaim God's love and grace offered to people without requirement or prerequisite. He had many valued companions who gave him prayer, resources, and support. And this included many women, which illustrated his true value of their worth in his ministry and in the church. He struggled with his own dubious past, his sinfulness, with physical, mental, and spiritual weakness, and with how others viewed and received him. And he professed a reliance on God's grace and the hope of resurrection above his own abilities or lack thereof.

What many find appealing about The Doctor, I also find interesting about Paul's life and ministry. Both have great knowledge and experience but also struggle with their limitations. They both have incredible wisdom to offer their respective universes and they've inspired so many others to be their best selves, but they have each failed to get it right at times as well. That both of them can be so human while also being elevated to such a high status is fascinating to me, and that's what I was most interested in as I wrote. They each have done incredible things, sometimes despite themselves.

If nothing else, I hope that that humanity can be its own access point for delving more deeply into one or both of these figures. Both The Doctor and Paul can teach us so much about living according to kindness, peace, inclusion, valuing diversity, and compassion. And for Christians, we may need a new way of seeing how doing so as possible.

During The Second Doctor's first adventure in "Power of the Daleks," he at one point expresses admiration for one of his companions, Polly, by saying, "I like her. She's curious."

May the grace-filled gifts of God always inspire in us curiosity about faith, life, and the universe, as both The Doctor and the Apostle each intended in their own way.

Bibliography

Achtemeier, Paul. *Romans*. Interpretation. Louisville: John Knox, 1985.

Borg, Marcus, and John Dominic Crossan. *The First Paul: Reclaiming the Radical Visionary Behind the Church's Conservative Icon*. New York: HarperOne, 2009.

Evans, Rachel Held. *Searching for Sunday: Loving, Leaving, and Finding the Church*. Nashville: Thomas Nelson, 2015.

———. *A Year of Biblical Womanhood: How a Liberated Woman Found Herself Sitting on Her Roof, Covering Her Head, and Calling Her Husband 'Master'*. New York: Thomas Nelson, 2012.

Horsley, Richard. *1 Corinthians*. Abingdon New Testament Commentaries. Nashville: Abingdon, 1998.

Lewis, C. S. *The Screwtape Letters*. New York: Simon and Schuster, 1996.

Meeks, Wayne. *The First Urban Christians: The Social World of the Apostle Paul*. New Haven, CT: Yale University, 1983.

Nelson, Jeffrey A. *Wonder and Whiskey: Insights on Faith from the Music of Dave Matthews Band*. Eugene, OR: Wipf & Stock, 2018.

Roetzel, Calvin. *2 Corinthians*. Abingdon New Testament Commentaries. Nashville: Abingdon, 2007.

Rohr, Richard. *Eager to Love: The Alternative Way of Francis of Assisi*. Cincinnati: Franciscan, 2014.

Sampley, J. Paul. "The First Letter to the Corinthians." In *The New Interpreter's Bible*, edited by Leander E. Keck et al., 10:771–1003. Nashville: Abingdon, 2002.

———. "The Second Letter to the Corinthians." In *The New Interpreter's Bible*, edited by Leander E. Keck et al., 11:1–180. Nashville: Abingdon, 2000.

Spencer, F. Scott. "Aquila and Priscilla." In *The New Interpreter's Bible Dictionary*, edited by Katharine Doob Sakenfeld et al., 1:211. Nashville: Abingdon, 2006.

———. "Barnabas." In *The New Interpreter's Bible Dictionary*, edited by Katharine Doob Sakenfeld et al., 1:399. Nashville: Abingdon, 2006.

Stendahl, Krister. *Paul Among Jews and Gentiles*. Philadelphia: Fortress, 1976.

Thiselton, Anthony. "Chloe." In *The New Interpreter's Bible Dictionary*, edited by Katharine Doob Sakenfeld et al., 1:594. Nashville: Abingdon, 2006.

Vallely. Paul. "Vicar Struggles to Forgive the Terrorists Who Killed Her Daughter." *The Independent*, March 7, 2006. https://www.independent.co.uk/news/uk/this-britain/vicar-struggles-to-forgive-the-terrorists-who-killed-her-daughter-6107339.html.

Volf, Miroslav. *Exclusion and Embrace: A Theological Exploration of Identity, Otherness, and Reconciliation*. Nashville: Abingdon, 1996.

Wright, N. T. "The Letter to the Romans." In *The New Interpreter's Bible*, edited by Leander E. Keck et al., 10:393–770. Nashville: Abingdon, 2002.